France

A Woof Guide

By
Paul Wojnicki

About the author

Paul Wojnicki is a freelance journalist and novelist. He holds a degree in literature from the Open University and post graduate qualifications from Edge Hill University. He has spent the last seventeen years travelling every continent in the world and has been travelling with his dog Falco since 2010.

This first edition published in Sept 2013

Contents

The Pet Passport Scheme

Recent changes to the Pet Passport scheme mean that it's now even easier to take your pet to countries within the EU, especially if you have a car.

The scheme originally required rabies vaccinations and expensive blood tests before travelling. Then tick and tapeworm treatments between 24-48 hours of returning to the UK. This meant meticulous planning was required before and during the trip. Since 2012 however the rules have been somewhat relaxed, meaning that the blood tests and the narrow window in which to get treatments are now a thing of the past.

These days it's a simple matter of getting a rabies vaccination (every three years) then making sure your dog is treated for tapeworm by a registered vet between 24 and 120 hours of returning to the UK.

Your dog will of course need a microchip to identify them and validate the passport as belonging to them, but most of us have our friends micro-chipped anyway. The important thing to remember is to get your dog chipped before having the rabies vaccination. You'll find a checklist in the steps below.

Step 1- Get your dog micro-chipped.

If you already have a microchip then this one will do just fine, the important thing is that the passport can be assigned to the dog (sorry but passport photographs are not valid).

Step 2- Get a rabies vaccination.

This should cost somewhere in the region of £30-50 and will last for three years. Please note that you must have the vaccination **after** the dog has been micro-chipped.

Step 3- Wait 3 weeks.

You'll have to wait 21 days after the original vaccination before you can **return to** the UK. This only applies to returning to the UK, so you can have the vaccination a week before travelling **out** of the UK if you plan to stay for two weeks. After the first vaccination and waiting period, you can enter the UK whenever you like as long as booster vaccinations are given on time and you continue to meet the other entry requirements.

Step 4- Ask your vet for a pet passport.

You'll no doubt have told your vet that you're having the rabies vaccination for a pet passport, you can ask them for a pet passport at the same time or at a later date. The passport stays valid as long as you continue to meet the entry requirements.

Step 5- Have a great holiday.

Don't forget to read your Woof Guide first, so you know exactly where you want to go and what you want to see. And don't forget that you'll need to use an **approved route** to come home. This is actually not as bad as it sounds as **all the ferry companies and Eurotunnel are approved routes.** Unfortunately for those without cars Eurostar does not carry animals at this moment in time.

Step 6- Tapeworm treatment.

You'll need to have him/her treated for tapeworm by a registered vet before returning to the UK. These are often the same tablets that we treat them with at home.

The important thing is that the vet stamps your pet passport to say that the dog was treated **no less than 24 hours and no more than 120 hours before returning to the UK.** That's between 1 and 5 days if your math is as bad as mine.

Step 7- Come home.

Remember that all of the approved transport companies will require you to book in at an animal transport centre before departure to confirm that you've had all the appropriate treatments administered. Try to arrive at the port in good time to do this and check individual requirements when booking your transport.

Getting there

The biggest concern for most of us is, "how will my dog be transported?" For this reason, as well as economic reasons we have omitted air travel as a method of travelling to France. That's not to say it can't be done, but the cost alone would be around £1,000 and the stress to you and your dog just doesn't make it a cost effective or worthwhile option (unless you happen to own a private jet).

By far the least stressful option (at least as far as your dog is concerned), is the Channel Tunnel, closely followed by the shorter cross-channel ferries in which the dog stays in a (presumably) familiar car. Though there are other options, such as the P&O's North Sea route from Hull to Zeebrugge (a good option for people in the north of England travelling to the north east of France), and Brittany Ferries Cap Finistère service from Portsmouth to Bilbao (which is handy for the south west of France and boasts pet friendly cabins to minimise distress for owners and pets alike).

Eurotunnel

Folkestone-Calais
One way September 10th 2013, from £60.
Ten day return September 10th-20th 2013, from £120.

About the crossing
Eurotunnel is without doubt the quickest and the least stressful crossing for you and your dog. Your dog stays with you, the crossing only takes 35 minutes and there are no muzzle, leash or kennel requirements. You simply drive onto the train, sit in your car for 35 minutes and then drive off again in France. It's also the only cross channel option that doesn't rely on the weather.
Unfortunately if you don't have a car then this option is unavailable. It also costs more than twice the amount charged by P&O and DFDS for their Dover to Calais sailings on the same dates in our price comparison, but at £60 each way for a ten day trip in September 2013 it represents excellent value for money and a hassle free way of reaching the continent. Dogs cost £15 each way, per pet.

Website: www.eurotunnel.com

P&O Ferries

Dover to Calais
One way September 10th 2013, from £25.
Ten day return September 10th-20th 2013, from £50.

About the crossing
If you're taking your pet(s) on the Dover-Calais route you will need to check-in at least one hour before departure and the animals must remain inside the vehicle at all times during the crossing. **Foot passengers cannot travel with pets.** P&O charge £15 each way per animal at the time of writing.

With fares starting at £50 return for a ten day trip this crossing is possibly the cheapest way to reach France. It's also one of the faster crossings with crossing times as short as ninety minutes.

Website: www.poferries.com

DFDS Seaways/LD Lines

Dover-Calais
One way, September 10th 2013, from £19.
Ten day return September 10th-20th 2013, from £38.
Dover-Dunkurque
One way September 10th 2013, from £19
Ten day return September 10th-20th 2013, from £38
Newhaven-Dieppe
One way September 10th 2013, from £39
Ten day return September 10th-20th 2013, from £78
Portsmouth-Le Havre
One way September 10th 2013, from £90
Ten day return September 10th-20th 2013, from £142

About the crossing
Foot passengers wishing to travel to France with their pets have to book via the call centre.

Animals are required to stay in your vehicle for the duration of the crossing.

There is a charge of £30.00 / €36.00 for animals travelling in to the UK direction, (no charge from the UK to France). A DFDS Seaways representative will carry out all checks on your pet.

Website: www.dfdsseaways.co.uk

My Ferry Link

Dover-Calais
One way, September 10th 2013, from £29.
Ten day return September 10th-20th 2013, from £58.

About the crossing
Animals are required to stay in your vehicle for the duration of the crossing.
There is a charge of £25.00 for animals travelling in to the UK direction, (no charge from the UK to France).
Website: www.myferrylink.com

Brittany Ferries

Portsmouth to Caen 6-7 hours, from £119 each way, dogs stay in car.
Portsmouth to Cherbourg 3 hours, from £139 each way, dogs stay in car.
Portsmouth to Le Havre 3 hours 45, from £159 each way, dogs stay in car.
Portsmouth to St-Malo 9-10¾ hours, from £244 one way, dogs stay in kennels.
Poole to Cherbourg 3¾ hours, from £139 each way, dogs stay in car.
Plymouth to Roscoff 6-8 hours, from £169 each way, dogs stay in kennels.

About the crossing
Kennels are situated on Deck 10 on the Plymouth-Roscoff service with a dedicated area adjacent to the kennels for exercise and comfort breaks. This is open-air. Pets on this service can also remain in vehicles and there are set times for you to visit the garage to exercise and toilet them.
The kennels on the Portsmouth-St Malo service are situated forward of the garage on Deck 5 where a small exercise area is provided. Dogs can be left in your vehicle if you wish. Pet visits are at 12:00 and 15:00 on a day sailing and 22:00 on an overnight sailing.
Other vessels do not have kennels and all animals remain in your vehicle. Visits to exercise your pet and allow them a comfort break are made by arrangement

with staff at the Information Desk onboard. Visits to the garage on high speed services are not permitted.

Please note the kennels are not available when the ships operate to/from Caen, Cherbourg or *Roscoff. (*Except for **Pont-Aven** crossings from Plymouth to Roscoff on Thursday nights.)

When travelling on Bretagne to St Malo it is not compulsory to use the kennels, your dog(s) may stay in your vehicle.

Website: www.brittanyferries.com

Condor Ferries

Portsmouth to Cherbourg 5 ½ hours, £107 each way, dogs stay in car.
Poole (or Weymouth) to St-Malo 5-7 hours, £106 each way, dogs stay in car.

About the crossing
Pets are charged £30 for the first pet, and £15 per subsequent pet when travelling on a return journey from the UK to St Malo, Portsmouth to Cherbourg and vice versa. This service is only valid for pets travelling within a vehicle and is not valid for those travelling as foot passengers.
Pets must be left in the vehicle during the crossing.
Visits to the car deck during the journey are only permitted when accompanied by a member of the ship's crew, and are dependent on weather conditions.
The ferries travel to France via the Channel Islands.

Website: www.condorferries.co.uk

Alternate crossings

P&O Ferries

Hull-Zebrugge- An interesting option for travellers in the north of England. The ferry leaves Hull every night at 18:30 (returning at 19:00) and arrives in Zeebrugge (close to the French border) at around 08:00 the following day. The kennels are clean and spacious and the cabins provide a relaxing alternative to driving south for several hours. This route also allows foot passengers to travel with a dog. The downside to this route is leaving your dog in the onboard kennels overnight.

Brittany ferries

Portsmouth-Bilbao- A really good alternative if you're planning to visit the south west (or even the west coast) of France. Bilbao is around 1 hr 40 minutes drive from Biarritz in the south west of France and the ferry is a relaxing alternative to driving there. The prices may seem a little steep at first glance but once you factor in the tolls and a cross channel ferry this option is very cost effective indeed. What's more, the (limited) pet friendly cabins on this service provide a stress free way to get there for all concerned.

Foot passengers

At the time of writing there are only really three viable ways of crossing to the continent as a foot passenger. The first is with LD Lines from Portsmouth to Le Havre, the second is with P&O from Hull to Zeebrugge, which is relatively close to France and the third is from Harwich to Amsterdam. It is possible to travel from Amsterdam to Paris by direct train, which takes 3 hours and 17 minutes (from €30) and from Bruges (close to Zeebrugge) to Paris in 2 hours and 26 minutes (from €40).

Getting Around

Rail

Even if you arrive in France by car it's often worth using the train to get around. As long as you book ahead and use the right websites then it's possible to travel from Dieppe in the north of the country to Marseille in the south for around £30 per person, and that's with a free stopover in Paris.

However France has a rail system almost as confusing as the UK's. The main thing to remember is that there are basically three websites to visit if you want to travel by train. It's important when travelling with anything but the smallest of dogs to try ouigo.com or idtgv.com first (wherever possible) as these are the only sites you'll be able to pre-book your dog on.

ouigo.com

In 2013, SNCF launched a budget rail service called ouigo.com. The service operates from Marne la Vallée (Disney) just outside Paris to a limited number of destinations: Lyon, Aix en Provence, Avignon, Marseille, Nimes & Montpelier. The seats are comfortable and reasonably spacious but there is no first class and you have to pay for baggage separately (€5). That said you can buy tickets from the outskirts of Paris to the south of France for as little as €10 per person each way.

It's also possible to pre-book dogs for a set fee of €30 each way (for pets over 6kg, free otherwise).

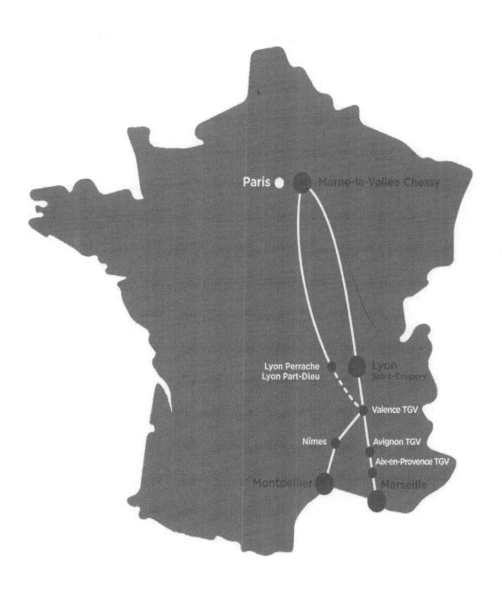

Paris ● ○ Marne-la-Vallée Chessy

Lyon Perrache
Lyon Part-Dieu ● ● Lyon
Saint-Exupéry

Valence TGV

Nîmes ● ● Avignon TGV

Aix-en-Provence TGV

Montpellier ● ● Marseille

IDTGV bills itself as a new way to travel by train, with 100% online booking, low fares and two distinctive styles: iDZAP for passengers who want to socialise, and iDZEN for a quiet, more relaxing trip. The fares are generally lower than other TGV trains and dogs can be pre-booked for €35 each way regardless of distance or regular fare. There is a wider selection of trains and destinations than Ouigo, but not as comprehensive as voyages-sncf.com.

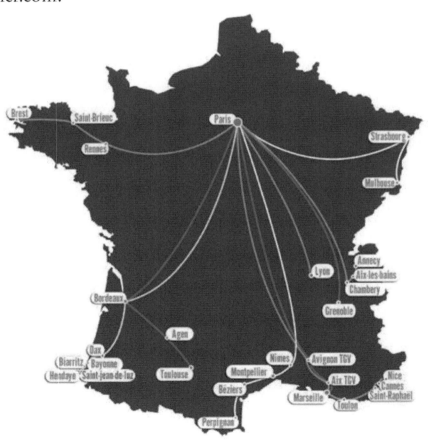

All routes except Ouigo, are available for purchase on voyages-sncf.com but dogs cannot be pre-booked on this website. So if your dog weighs more than 6kg then you'll need to buy a ticket for him/her on the platform, which costs 50% of regular fare (not 50% of discounted fares). Be sure to buy your own tickets online as the prices are often much better if you book ahead.

Intercités de nuit

Intercités de nuit are night services running to the south of France. The Lunéa might be of particular interest to dog owners without vehicles. This is a night train with several services to destinations on the south east and south west of France. Examples include Biarritz (10 hrs 30, from €65) and Nice (11 hrs 30, from €65). You can book out a full couchette if you want to avoid offending other passengers.

By Road

France has a superb road network. The country has an area roughly twice that of Britain but with only slightly more people, so for the most part traffic is rarely a problem (though this might not be the case at peak holiday times).

If you're in a hurry take the excellent motorways, known as A roads or Autoroutes which can easily speed you from one side of France to the other in a long day, though the tolls can soon add up on these routes.

The French highway network is run by several private companies, which is why they are not free. The multiple tolls on the French autoroutes can be paid by credit card and cash. There are also specific subscriptions and magnetic travel cards which are of more use to lorry drivers and commuters than tourists.

Alternatively follow the yellow roads for some enjoyable driving and a taste of the real France (Michellin road maps, or a decent sat nav will be able to keep you to these roads).

Tip: If you want to calculate a journey time, toll costs or estimate fuel costs use www.viamichelin.co.uk.

Routes in blue depict toll roads

Paris

Getting there
Road
Calais- 3 hrs, Dunkurque- 3 hrs, Dieppe- 2 hrs 10, Le Havre- 2 hrs-10, St-Malo- 4 hrs, Roscoff- 5 hrs 20, Cherbourg- 3 hrs 30, Caen- 2 hrs 20.

Rail
Calais- 1 hr 45 (€45), Dunkurque- 2 hrs (€45), Dieppe- 2 hrs 10(€45), Le Havre- 2 hrs 10(€33.50), St-Malo- 3 hrs (€70), Roscoff- 4 hrs 45 (€75), Cherbourg- 3 hrs 15 (€50), Caen- 2 hrs 15 (€35).

All prices shown are based on the standard second class fare, you can usually pick tickets up for much less if you book in advance and stick to the time on the ticket. Dogs cannot be pre-booked on most trains and are charged at 50% of the standard second class fare, even if you travel in first class. Pets weighing less than 6kg travel for €6, provided they are in a carry bag or basket.

Get around
If the thought of driving in Paris is a nightmare then parking will be your *worst* nightmare. It's *always* best to avoid driving in central Paris (either by staying in a hotel on the outskirts, or leaving your car there in a secure car park and reaching your hotel by train). But if you *must* drive into the centre of Paris try to find a hotel, with parking, that's close to an RER station and use the RER to get around.

Small dogs can be taken on buses, trams, Metro and the

RER. Larger dogs, with the exception of guide dogs, are officially banned from the **Metro** but you'll see them all the same. As long as you are travelling outside of rush-hour, it's unlikely you'll have a problem.

Large dogs are not *officially* allowed on the trams or buses but they can be taken on the **RER** if they're on a leash and muzzled with a half price ticket for the dog, the same tickets you would buy for a child.

See & Do

Dogs in Paris live very sophisticated lives. They are welcomed in many bakeries, cafes, shops and bars. But rather bizarrely most parks have large signs saying *no dogs - even on a leash* "pas de chien, même tenus en laisse".

Fortunately in Paris most rules are not strictly enforced and Parisians seem to adopt the attitude that "rules don't apply to me or my dog". Also leash laws, where they exist are completely ignored. You'll see plenty of well behaved dogs walking with no leash.

That said, you are unlikely to be allowed into museums and theatres with your dog and so will have to contend yourself with visiting one of the many world famous landmarks instead. A few of the more well known landmarks are listed below.

Arc de Triomphe - The Arc de Triomphe exudes grandeur and offers a central view of the city Métro/**RER** *Charles de Gaulle-Etoile* (1, 2, 6, A).

Château de Versailles- France's most exquisite château, on the outskirts of the city and easily visited by RER train **Versailles Rive Gauche station, (C line)**. Once the home to Louis XVI and Marie Antoinette. You can bring small dogs into the world famous gardens (which really have to be seen to be believed). Larger dogs are welcome in the adjacent park area.

The *Eiffel Tower (Tour Eiffel)*- No other monument symbolises Paris more than the tower. **RER *Champ de Mars-Tour Eiffel* (C line)** has a station close by. Dogs are not allowed up the tower but there is plenty of grass to enjoy a picnic and a photo opportunity underneath.

Notre Dame Cathedral- A hugely impressive Gothic cathedral that was also the inspiration for Victor Hugo's novel *The Hunchback of Notre Dame*. Take the **RER *(lines B and C) to Saint-Michel-Notre Dame.***

Pantheon- Located in the 5th arrondissement on the Montagne Sainte-Geneviève, the Panthéon looks out over all of Paris and one of the most important architectural achievements of its time. This is the final resting place of great heroes of the French Republic such as Voltaire, Victor Hugo, and Marie Curie. **RER line B, *Luxembourg.***

Sacré Coeur-A church perched on top of the highest point in Paris. Behind the church is the artists' area, in front are spectacular views of the whole city. There is no RER station close to **Sacré Coeur but** you can walk from Gare du Nord (10 mins) or run the (albeit very low) risk on the Métro. Station *Anvers* (line 2) or *Abbesses* (line 12), then climb the stairs on Rue Foyatier or take the funicular to the top of the hill.

The Louvre- Of course you won't be allowed inside the museum with a dog, but sitting outside people watching next to the famous glass pyramid is one of *the* things to do in Paris (walk from **Chatelet Les Halles on line RER A**).

Walk along the Seine- A great way to see some of Paris' best landmarks is to stroll along the Seine. Start at the Eiffel Tower and pass the Louvre and Place de la Concorde on your way to Notre Dame and Saint-Chapelle. You'll pass flea markets and artists along the bank, or stop off to people watch at one of the many cafes along the way.

Tuilleries Gardens- Allows dogs on the two elevated areas overlooking the gardens. The northern dog area faces the Rue de Rivoli and the southern overlooks the Seine River. Once again signs say that dogs should be on a leash but if your dog is well behaved this rule is pretty much ignored.

Sleep

There are literally hundreds of pet friendly hotels in Paris. Chain hotels that readily accept pets include Novotel, ibis, Mercure, Campanile, Holiday Inn and Comfort.

For your convenience we've only listed hotels that are close to an RER station and/or have parking on site or nearby.

If you're looking for something a little different try visiting the hotel section on kayak.co.uk or Trip Advisor and filter the results to include pets.

Gare du Nord area

Paris Gare du Nord Château Landon, *197-199 rue La Fayette 75010-* Located just a few minutes walk from the Gare du Nord RER station makes this hotel extremely convenient. Rooms are, as you'd expect from the ibis chain, small but clean and presentable. It's fine for a one night stay but not somewhere to stay for a full week, unless you only plan to sleep at the hotel (from €90).

Best Western Albert Premier, *162 Rue La Fayette, 75010-* Clean, comfortable rooms close to the RER station. Rooms have bath as well as a shower and tea and coffee facilities, so probably a little more upmarket than the ibis, though still with small rooms from €110).

Versailles Area

ibis Château de Versailles, *4 Avenue du General de Gaulle, 78000-* The location for a visit to the palace couldn't be better and it's a short walk to the RER sta tion for the rest of Paris. The rooms are typically small but clean (from €100).

Pullman Versailles Château, *2 Bis Avenue de Paris, 78000 Versailles-* A well placed, upmarket hotel with a price to match. The location is a few hundred metres from the forecourt of the Château, and the RER station (Rive Gauche). The rooms are pleasant and comfortable; some of them overlook the palace while others overlook old Versailles (from €160).

Gentilly Area

ibis Paris Porte d'Italie, *13 rue du Val de Marne, 94250 Gentilly-* If you're on a budget you might want to consider staying somewhere like Gentilly. The location of this hotel isn't amazing but it's only a few minutes' walk from Gentilly RER station so you can get into the centre easily. As with all ibis hotels the rooms aren't enormous but are decent enough to have a shower and a good rest after a busy day exploring Paris (from €50).

Eiffel Tower area

Auteuil Tour Eiffel, *8-10 rue Felicien David, 75016 Paris-* In a very good location, around a mile walk from the tower and close to the RER station. Slightly dated rooms but reasonably spacious for Paris. Breakfast is included and the staff are polite and friendly. Also has parking (rooms from €125).

Ramada Paris Tour Eiffel, *102 Bd de Grenelle, 75015 Paris-* Clean comfortable rooms that are fairly spacious (by Parisian standards). It's around 10 minutes walk from the tower and a similar distance from the RER station (from €135).

ibis Paris Tour Eiffel Cambronne, *2 rue Cambronne, 15th Arr. 75015-* Typically small and clean rooms, some of which have a view of the tower. The tower is around a 10 minute walk from the hotel as is the RER station (from €100).

Gare de Lyon Area

Best Western Aurore, *13 Rue Traversiere, 75012 Paris-* Set in a surprisingly quiet location to say it is only minutes from Gare de Lyon. Perfect for onward travel to South France. Staff are friendly and helpful. Rooms, as always in Paris, are very small but clean and tidy (from €90).

Marne La Vallee/ Val d'Europe/Disney

If you don't mind staying out of town Val d'Europe/Disneyland Paris is an excellent budget option with the added advantage of avoiding a drive in and around central Paris. There are lots of hotels in the area, often at half the price of a city centre hotel. There are two RER stations, Val d'Europe and Marne-la-Vallee/Chessy. The Chessy station also has a TGV station, ideal for travelling to southern France.

Vets
Gare du Nord

Cabinet Veterinary Doctor Bobbelaere, *9 Rue Perdonnet, 75010. Tel: +33 1 46 07 69 75.*

Versailles
Clinical Veterinary Villemin, *79 Parish Street, 78000 Versailles. Tel: +33 1 39 50 00 89.*

Gentilly
Laillet Béatrice, *1 Rue Aristide Briand 94250 Gentilly. Tel: +33 1 45 46 26 39.*

Eiffel Tower
Clinique Vétérinaire du Docteur Jean-Michel Rabany, *117 Rue Saint-Dominique 75007, Paris. Tel: +33 1 47 05 48 67.*

Gare de Lyon
Clinique Vétérinaire St Antoine, *61 Rue Crozatier, 75012 Paris. Tel: +33 1 43 43 17 13.*

Disneyland Paris

While Disney only allows guide dogs and service dogs for the visually impaired into its park, it does have the **Animal Care Centre**, a kennels facility located between the main Disney Parks' parking lot and the esplanade to Disney Village, at the top of the moving walkways. Here, your dog will be cared for with food and water for the duration of your stay. Rates are charged per day and differ for each type of animal.

Note that the Animal Care Centre crew are not permitted to walk dogs, so you should return to the centre during your stay to ensure they are given a chance for some exercise.

Dogs must be micro chipped and have proof of rabies vaccination; however the rules can differ to the pet passport so check with the Animal Care Centre on how recent the rabies vaccination has to be before booking expensive park tickets.

Contact Details

Be sure to contact the Animal Care Centre directly for further enquiries, questions and advice, *Tel: 00 33 1 64 74 28 73.*

Getting there

Disneyland has a dog friendly RER station called Marne-la-Vallee/Chessy that is served by line A4. Trains run every 15 minutes until midnight and take about 40 minutes from central Paris. By road take the A4 and exit at junction 14. There is also a direct TGV from Lille (1 hr 20, from €20) and an indirect service from Calais (2 hrs, from €33).

See & Do

Disneyland Paris- While leaving your dog in a kennels facility defeats the object taking him or her on holiday with you in the first place, you might have kids (or adults) who dream of nothing more than visiting Disneyland. If that's the case then the Animal Care Facility makes it possible to do this without leaving them in a kennels overnight.

Take a train to central Paris- Around 40 minutes away by RER is the world famous City of Light.

Lake de Serris- Around half a mile away from the Disney Village and close to the Val d'Europe is a small pleasant lake where dogs are welcome to walk and swim.

Take a train south- If you'd like to travel to the south of France but just can't face the drive or afford the toll roads the Marne la Vallee TGV station is the cheapest way of getting there. With fares to Montpellier and Nimes starting at just €10 each way this makes an excellent place to leave the car and hop on a train south for a couple of days (or weeks).

Sleep

ibis Marne la Vallée Val d'Europe, *2 Place Jean Monnet, 77144 Montévrain*- Right next to the Val d'Europe RER station and one stop from Disney. Typical ibis rooms clean and comfortable and slightly larger than some of the other ibis rooms in Paris. Also next to the huge shopping centre if you need to purchase food for yourself or the dog (from €60).

Vets

Dr Delphine LACAZE, *Dr Jean-Pierre LEROUX -6, Boulevard Thibaud de Champagne. Tel: +33 01 64 66 84 84.*

A 4-legs-Doctors Vets, *11 D Street Courtalin, 77700 Magny-le-Hongre. Tel: +33 1 60 04 16 16.*

The North

Calais

Getting there
Eurotunnel- Folkestone 35 mins (from £52 each way, based on 5 days or less).
Ferry- (P&O, DFDS, My Ferry Link), Dover 1 hr 30 (from £19 each way).

See & Do
Calais Town Hall (Hôtel de Ville)- Calais' finest landmark is a gorgeous piece of Flemish architecture with a towering belfry that can be seen for miles around.
Rodin's Six Burghers- At the foot of the clock tower and the town hall stands a monument to the bravery of six local citizens who held off the siege of Calais until starvation eventually forced the city to parley for surrender. Edward offered to spare the people of the city if any six of its top leaders would surrender themselves to him, presumably to be executed. Edward demanded that they walk out wearing nooses around their necks, and carrying the keys to the city and castle. Although the burghers expected to be executed, their lives were spared by the intervention of England's Queen, Philippa of Hainault, who persuaded her husband to exercise mercy by claiming that their deaths would be a bad omen for her unborn child.
Calais lighthouse- A 51 metre lighthouse with a grassy area in front ideal for exercising a dog.

Beaches- There are at least 5 dog friendly beaches stretching from Calais to the west and another three toward Dunkirk. Bleriot Plage is a stretch of pristine white sand that would be packed with tourists if it were in the UK. Yet on a mild day you can virtually have the place to yourself and even on a fine summer day you'll have more than enough space for walking together and soaking up the rays as the ferries sail by.

Set between Calais and Boulogne the Côte d'Opale is a series of cliffs, rolling sand dunes and wide beaches backed by farmland for approximately 40km. You'll even find the (often graffiti covered) remains of the Nazi gun emplacements and fortifications along the coast. You'll need a car to visit the area but you'll find plenty of dog friendly beaches along the route. You can see five of them on the map below.

Sleep
Hotel Kyriad Calais Sud Coquelles, *Avenue Charles De Gaulle, 62231 Coquelles*- Perfectly adequate for a stopover, small rooms but clean and well situated for the tunnel and ferry (from €35).

Cottage Hotel, *648 Rue de Tunis, 62100 Calais*- Another hotel that's ideal for a stopover with clean rooms, friendly staff and a good location for the ferries, beaches and tunnel. There is a restaurant and bar on site that were happy to let our dog sit with us (from €45).

Holiday Inn Calais Coquelles, *Avenue Charles de Gaulle, 62231 Calais*- Good sized rooms and bathrooms though a little dated now. There are plenty of facilities onsite such as a pool, sauna and a hot tub (rooms from €60).

Vets

Dr Christiane Petry, *1148 Bvd General de Gaulle, Nord-Pas-de-Calais 62100. Tel: +33 3 21 34 77 39.*

Clinic Veterinaire du Parc, *73 Rue Aristide Briand, Nord-Pas-de-Calais, 62100. Tel: +33 3 21 34 93 88.*

Bernard Alcouffe Centre Vet, *139 Bvd Curie, Nord-Pas-de-Calais 62100. Tel: +33 3 21 82 15 11.*

Lille

With an attractive old town crisscrossed by cobbled streets and the grand Place General-de-Gaulle, Lille has to be one of the most underrated large cities in France. It's also a great place to leave the car and explore the rest of France by rail, with direct services to many parts of France (Lyon 3 hrs, Nantes 4 hrs, and Marseille 5 hrs).

Getting there
Car- Calais-1 hr 20, Dieppe- 2 hrs 30, Dunkirk 55mins.
Rail- Calais- 30 mins (€16.60), Dunkirk 1 hr (€15), Paris 1 hr (from €25).

See & Do
Old town- A fine old town full of restored 17th and 18th century houses.
Place du Général-de-Gaulle- The focal part of the city centre is better known as the "Grand Place". It is bordered by grand and historic buildings and has a central fountain and pillar on which a statue of a goddess stands.
Place Rihour- Surrounded by restaurants this square houses the tourist information centre inside its main attraction, the 15th century **Palais Rihour**.
The **town hall** is worth a look and can be combined nicely with a visit to the 17th century **Porte de Paris,** a grand arch and masterpiece of military art built to celebrate the victories of Louis XIV.
The Opera (built 1923) and the **Chamber of Commerce**

(built 1921) are located close together and offer magnificent sights, especially when lit-up at night.

Sleep
ibis Styles Lille Centre Gare Beffroi, *172 Rue de Paris, 59800 Lille–* Modern and brightly coloured chain hotel. Rooms aren't huge but are functional, clean & tidy. Excellent location for town centre and rail stations. Free tea/coffee making facilities in foyer (from €65).

Citadines Lille Centre, *83 Avenue Willy Brandt, Euralille, 59777 Lille-* Bright modern apartment style rooms with a basic kitchen if you'd rather prepare your own food. The location is perfect for the train station, restaurants and there's a Carrefour supermarket at the doorstep (from €80).

Crowne Plaza Lille, *335 Blvd de Leeds, 59777 Lille-* Right across the road from the Gare de Lille and only a ten minute walk from the centre of Lille. The rooms are spacious and comfortable as you'd expect from the prestigious chain. An excellent option if you can find a decent deal in advance (from €90).

Vets
Clinique Vétérinaire Jeanne d'Arc, *260 rue Solférino, 59000, Lille. Tel +33 3 20 40 79 82.*

Jean-Jacques Duyck, *260 Rue Solférino, 59000, Lille. Tel +33 3 20 40 79 82.*

Somme

Getting there

You'll need a car to visit the battlefields and cemeteries of the Somme as most cemeteries and battlefields are out of the main towns. Some of the major towns with battle sites nearby are:

Albert- Calais- 1 hr 40, Dieppe- 1 hr 45, Dunkirk- 1 hr 50, La Havre- 2 hrs 10, Lille- 1hr 10.

Arras- Calais- 1 hr 10, Dieppe- 2 hrs 15, Dunkirk- 1 hr 25, La Havre- 2 hrs 40, Lille- 40 mins.

Lens- Calais- 1 hr 05, Dieppe- 2 hrs 20, Dunkirk- 1 hr 10, La Havre- 2 hrs 45, Lille- 30 mins.

See & Do

Even though there are no official rules on visiting war graves, you are able to visit them with your dog. Just remember to be respectful at all times and keep him/her on a lead. Below is an extract of a reply from the War Graves Commission that outlines their policy on visiting with a dog:

Please note that the Commission does not have a written policy with regard to the admission of dogs to our cemeteries and memorial grounds. Of course, we do not condone visitors who allow their dogs to run free or leave a mess behind but we are, as I am sure you will appreciate, reliant upon the sensibilities of individuals to ensure their behaviour is appropriate to the environment and to the feelings and beliefs of other visitors. I hope this is explanatory and that your visit goes well.

It is highly recommended to purchase a good guide if you want to fully appreciate the Somme but if you just want a taste then some of highlights of the Somme are listed below:

Lochnagar Crater- In La Boisselle, a vast and impressive crater in open farm-land, left by a tremendous explosion in the opening moments of the Battle of the Somme on 1 July 1916.

Beaumont-Hamel Newfoundland Memorial- Three miles north of **Albert** this vast preserved battlefield is dedicated to the Newfoundland forces killed during World War I. The memorial park is set on the site where the Newfoundland Regiment made an unsuccessful attack on the first day of the Battle of the Somme. It was the regiment's first major engagement and during an assault that lasted approximately 30 minutes the regiment was all but wiped out. The land was purchased in 1921 by the people of Newfoundland, the memorial site is the largest battalion memorial on the Western Front, and the largest area of the Somme battlefield that has been preserved. Along with preserved trench lines, there are a number of memorials and cemeteries contained within the site.

Vimy Ridge- Six miles south-west of **Lens**, Vimy Ridge saw almost two full years of fierce trench fighting before being recaptured by the Canadian forces. It's a massive site donated by France to the Canadian people in honour of their sacrifice. Because the land has been partially preserved with craters and trenches still in place, this is one of *the* best places to come to gain an insight into the realities of trench warfare. It's best to park near the pre-served trenches, the car park is a two minute stroll from them but dogs are not allowed in this area. You can then walk your dog around the rest of the area, passing old trenches and craters as you walk toward the monument. Visitors are warned not to stray from the paths because unexploded ordinance still lies there.

Sleep
If you can't find a reasonably priced hotel in Lens, Arras or Albert, try staying in Lille which is only around 30 minutes to an hour from all three towns.
Holiday Inn Express Arras, *3 Rue Docteur Brassart, 62000 Arras*- Good clean rooms that are generously sized and come with plenty of tea and coffee making facilities. The hotel is only five minutes away from the main square and train station. There is a free breakfast but underground parking costs €11 a day (rooms from €80).
ibis Albert, *Parc d'Activite Henri Potez, 80300 Albert*- Easy to find and central to a number of WWI sites. Clean, comfortable and reasonably spacious rooms. The hotel has free WIFI and a computer in the lobby that guests can use (from €65).
Le 33, *33 Rue Gambetta, 62300 Lens*- This B&B is situated in a quiet side street right in the town centre and is ideal as a base to visit the area. The rooms are spacious and very clean and a welcome change if you're bored of chain hotels. Breakfast is good but served communally at a large table (from €70).

Vets

Pinaud bored Tison SCP, *22 Rue Gallieni, 80300 Albert. Tel +33 3 22 74 68 74.*

Delroisse-Petitprez Véronique, *16 Chemin Authuille 80300 Albert. Tel: +33 3 22 75 16 65.*

Clinique Vétérinaire du Docteur Dewulf Alain, *19 Place de la République 62300 Lens. Tel +33 3 21 67 66 93.*

Clinique Vétérinaire Lafayette, *10 Rue Abel Bergaigne 62000 Arras. Tel: +33 3 21 51 68 68.*

Worth a visit

Azincourt- Scene of the famous Battle of Agincourt, which took place on 25 October 1415 (Saint Crispin's Day). Henry V's victory against a far larger French army, crippled France and started a new period in the Hundred Years' War. The battle is notable for the use of the English longbow, which Henry used in very large numbers. It is also the centre-piece of the play Henry V, by William Shakespeare. You'll find the battlefield near present-day Azincourt, about 12km northeast of **Hesdin** off the D928. Agincourt Centre Historique Médiéval brings the battle to life. You'll also find a map with a circular drive around the battle lines. One hour drive from Calais.

Boulogne-sur-Mer- The lower town is unremarkable but above it rises a cobbled medieval quarter, or ville haute, with its old town walls and basilica. There are also beaches that you can take your dog to out of the main season. Thirty minutes drive from Calais.

Dunkerque is a lively port, near Calais, with a boat-filled harbour and a place forever engraved in British history. It was from these shores that the evacuation of Allied troops took place in 1940.

Normandy

Rouen

Situated on the River Seine, approximately 90 miles northwest of Paris, Rouen is the capital of Upper Normandy. The ancient city where Joan of Arc was burned at the stake has been meticulously rebuilt after being destroyed several times over the centuries.

Getting there
Rail- Paris- 1 hr 30 (€10), Dieppe- 45 mins (€11), Le Havre- 55 mins (€15), Caen- 2 hrs (€26).
Car- Paris- 1 hr 30 minutes, Dieppe- 50 mins, Calais- 2 hrs, Le Havre- 1 hr 10, Caen- 1 hr 30.

See & Do
Eglise Jeanne d'Arc- A modern church dedicated to Joan of Arc, built beside the field in which see was burned to death.
Notre Dame Cathedral- A huge building dating back to the 4th Century. A spire built in the 19th Century meant that it was as the tallest building in the world for a short time. In the summer the city puts on a light show at night-times projecting Monet's cathedral paintings onto the facade of the building.

Sleep
Mercure Rouen Centre Cathedrale, *Angle rue St Nicolas et Rue Croix de Fer, 76000 Rouen*- Smack in the

middle of town, opposite the cathedral, unfortunately this makes it a little difficult to get to by car so use a Sat Nav. Very handy for the train station and with good sized comfortable rooms. Make sure you park on the second floor of the car park if you're in a larger car. Rooms from €99.

ibis Rouen Centre Rive Droite, *56 quai Gaston Boulet, 76000 Rouen-* Just over a kilometre from the cathedral and an easy walk along the river. The rooms are standard ibis size, clean and comfortable. There is a small park close to the hotel ideal for exercising a dog. Rooms from 60€.

Suite Novotel Rouen Normandie, *Quai Boisguilbert, 76000 Rouen-* Large, comfortable rooms with kettles and a microwave. Easy to find and park, approximately ten minutes walk from the centre. There's a grassy area and river nearby, ideal for exercising a dog. Rooms from 105€.

Vets

Veterinaire Laurant Marie, *7 Rue Alphonse-Samain, Eure, Haute-Normandie 27340. Tel: +33 2 35 23 19 88.*
Ringot Fabienne Danielle, *7 Rue Alsace Lorraine 76000 Rouen. Tel: +33 2 35 98 17 45.*

D–Day Beaches

Getting there
Ferry- Caen is the most convenient port for the D-Day beaches, but also longest of the ferry journeys. Le Havre and Cherbourg are probably better for dog owners. **Brittany Ferries** operate services to all three ports from **Portsmouth. Caen** 6-7 hours, from £119 each way (dogs stay in car). **Cherbourg** 3 hours, from £139 each way (dogs stay in car). **Le Havre** 3 hours 45, from £159 each way (dogs stay in car).
Rail- Paris (to Caen) 2 hrs (€19), Rouen (to Caen) 1 hr 45 (€26). Note that the bus routes covering most of the main landing beaches do not allow dogs. The closest beach to Caen is Sword Beach. You could take a taxi to Ouistreham (approx 10 miles), or a train to Bayeux and a taxi from here to Gold Beach (8 miles), which has a dog friendly section.
Car- Calais to Caen- 3 hrs 15, Le Havre to Caen-1 hr 10, Cherbourg to Caen- 1 hr 25, Paris to Caen- 2 hrs 30, Dieppe to Caen- 2 hrs. Note that the Cherbourg to Caen route passes most of the beaches in between.

See & Do
The beaches:
Sword Beach- The most easterly of the five beaches runs from Ouistreham to Luc-sur-Mer. The British landed at Sword Beach with a number of French commandos, who were given the honour of being in the first wave of the attack. Dogs can be exercised in many areas of the beach including Ouistreham and Luc-sur-

Mer.

Juno Beach- Invaded by the Canadians, the beach saw the greatest resistance after that at Omaha. St. Aubin-sur-Mer is a dog friendly beach and has a 50mm gun casement preserved at Place du Canada.

Gold Beach- The British landed on Gold Beach, which includes the resort of Arromanche-les-bains. There is a dog friendly section of beach here as well as it being the site of an incredible feat of engineering. The allies needed a port to bring in supplies. So they built concrete pontoons that were dragged across the channel and then sunk to form an artificial port. Twenty of the original pontoons still remain today.

Omaha Beach- Invaded by the US 29th Infantry Division this beach saw the greatest resistance of the D-Day landings partly because it was overlooked by bluffs 150 feet high that commanded the beaches and robbed the invasion of any real cover. These positions were also very well fortified and left undamaged by the allied bombing before the attacks. There are museums, monuments and cemeteries dedicated to the landing, as well as a dog friendly section of beach at St-Laurent-Sur-Mer.

Utah- Another beach invaded by the US. The town of Sainte-Mère-Église is probably the most famous D Day village of all because of the popularity of the film *The Longest Day*. The film depicted a paratrooper who snagged his lines on a church spire and was forced to watch as the battle raged below him. An effigy of the real life paratrooper, John Steele, still hangs from the church today. There is a dog friendly section of beach at Grand-camp-Maisy.

Sleep

Adagio Caen Centre, *1 Quai Eugene Meslin, 14000 Caen-* Very spacious apartment style rooms with well equipped kitchenettes. Clean and comfortable and close to the centre. Unfortunately at the time of writing there was no WIFI in the rooms, only in the lobby. Rooms from €90.

Hotel Le Bayeux, *9 Rue Tardif, 14400 Bayeux-* This three star hotel isn't fancy but has everything you need. It's clean, has a central location, friendly staff, speedy wireless internet and all for an excellent price. It's walking distance to cathedral and tapestry and a good base to explore the beaches from. Rooms from €50.

Vets

Clinique Vétérinaire, *1 Avenue du Colonel Dawson, 14150, Ouistreham. Tel: 02 31 96 55 82.*

Clinique Vétérinaire de Bayeux, *Rue de la Cambette 14400 Bayeux. Tel: +33 2 31 92 00 60.*

Clinique Vétérinaire Lefol Jean-François, *26 Rue Léon Lecornu 14000 Caen. Tel: +33 2 31 93 09 74.*

Mont St-Michel

Located on an island just off the coast of Lower Normandy Mont St-Michel is the site of the Norman Benedictine Abbey of St Michel, sitting on the peak of the rocky island and surrounded by the winding streets of a medieval town.

Dogs are not allowed into the abbey itself but the island and its cobbled streets with the abbey perched above them still makes for a wonderful trip.

Getting there
Car- Paris- 3 hrs 50, Calais- 4 hrs 30, Dieppe- 3 hrs, Le Havre- 2 hrs 20, Cherbourg- 2 hrs, Caen- 1 hr 20, St-Malo-50 mins.

Note- At the time of writing you could no longer park at the foot of the mount but had to park inland. There are electric buses running the kilometre or so to the mount, but technically you're not supposed to take your dog on board. That said, some people still do, but you'd be better off walking your dog there.

Rail- The nearest station is Pontorson from where there are buses running the 9km to the mont, dogs aren't supposed to be on the bus but many drivers turn a blind eye.

WARNING: Attempting to reach Mont Saint-Michel by any other route than the causeway can be dangerous, the deep mud and quicksand surrounding the island can kill and the water can sweep in quickly as the tide rises. It should only be crossed with an experienced guide and after checking the tide tables. Don't be tempted to let your dog off the leash as it could endanger you both.

See & Do

The abbey- The second most visited attraction in France, after the Eiffel Tower, and rightly so. Even from a distance it is a truly spectacular sight, floating like a mirage on the sea (or mudflats). The abbey began as a humble little monastery sitting on a rocky outcrop. Over the years medieval buildings sprung up around what would eventually become the most recognisable abbey in the country. During the Revolution the monastery served as a prison, but in 1966, exactly a thousand years after they first arrived the Benedictines were invited to return. They have since left again, replaced by monks and nuns from the Monastic Fraternity of Jerusalem.

The Island- Even though you won't be able to enter the abbey with a dog it's still worth visiting the island. Indeed only a minority climb high enough to reach the abbey itself at the summit; the rest stay in the picturesque, yet commercialised, medieval town lower down.

Sleep

Le Relais du Roy, *La Caserne BP 31, BP 8, F - 50170 Mont-St-Michel-* A very clean though slightly spartan hotel that is very close to Mont St. Michel (you actually have a view of it from some rooms). The beds are comfortable and spacious and there is free WIFI (rooms from €79).

Hotel Le Mouton Blanc, *Grande Rue | BP 18, 50170 Mont-St-Michel-* Spending the night *on* Mont St Michel is a special experience and there aren't many rooms on the island itself. Le Mouton Blanc however is set right on the spiralling street up to the abbey. Looking down onto the clamour below you can almost imagine yourself emptying a chamber pot onto their heads. Be aware that provisions being dragged up the cobbled streets might prevent a lie in the next morning (from €140).

Vets
Dr Guy Terwagne, *Rue Mont St Michel, 50170 Pontorson. Tel 02 33 60 21 23.*
Cabinet Vétérinaire St Michel, *6 Rue Saint-Michel 50170 Pontorson. Tel: +33 2 33 89 57 65.*

Worth a visit

Abbaye de Jumièges- About 15 miles west of Rouen sit haunting ruins of the abbey of Jumièges. The abbey has a long history of being destroyed (by the Vikings and during the revolution) and rebuilt. William the Conqueror actually attended the re-consecration, and if that's not history for you then I'm not sure what is.

Château Gaillard- Perched high above **Les Andelys**, around 25 miles south-east of Rouen, is the dramatic Château Gaillard. Built in 1196-97 under the auspices of Richard the Lionheart, it was later destroyed by Henry IV in the beginning of the 17th century. The dramatic ruins can be reached on foot via a steep path that leads off rue Richard-Coeur-de-Lion in **Petit Andely**.

Cherbourg- One of the Titanic's final ports and a mere 3 hours away from the UK, Cherbourg certainly makes an interesting port to arrive at in France. Its Old Town, close to the quay, is a maze of pedestrian alleys full of shops and restaurants.

Bayeux- Smaller, and more enjoyable to visit, than nearby Caen, Bayeux is famous for two cross channel invasions. The conquest of England by William the Conqueror began in Bayeux, and it was the first French city to be liberated in 1944, the day after D-Day. Indeed as well as housing the famous tapestry, it briefly became the capital of free France.

Brittany

St-Malo

One of Brittany's most famous attractions, the port of St-Malo oozes charm. A mast filled harbour, wonderful beaches and 17th century walls surrounding the old town. The walls were destroyed during the Second World War but painstakingly reconstructed afterward.

Getting there
Ferry- Brittany Ferries from Portsmouth, Condor Ferries from Weymouth and Poole.
Rail- Paris- 3 hrs.
Car- Calais 5 hrs, Cherbourg 2 hrs 30, Caen 1 hr 50, Le Havre 2 hrs 40.

See & Do
Walk on the ramparts- A walk along the ramparts will give you a fantastic view of the walled city as well as the sea and city beach.
Fort National- The remains of a former island prison can be seen from the city ramparts or walked across to at low tide. Dogs are allowed.
A stroll through the walled city is the perfect way to spend a few hours. The lively streets within the walls are packed with restaurants, bars and shops.
Beaches- The beaches are large and clean, but the closest beach that has an area reserved for dogs is at Dinard, just across the estuary 8 miles away.

Sleep

ibis Styles Saint-Malo Centre Historique, *4 Place du Poids du Roi, 35400 St-Malo-* Right next to the beaches and just inside the historic walls. Great for a short stay if you are using the ferry. Rooms are clean and comfortable and have large bathrooms. Parking near the hotel is €8 but there is free parking at the ferry port (a 10 minute walk away). Breakfast and unlimited WIFI are included in all rates. Rooms from €99.

La Villefromoy, *7 boulevard Hebert | Plage de Rochebonne, 35400 Saint-Malo-* A lovely small hotel, just one street back from the beach and promenade. The rooms are comfortable and beautifully decorated, with lovely bathrooms. It's a bit of a walk to the centre but the walk is along the front of the beach (from €90).

Kyriad Saint Malo Plage, *49 Chaussee du Sillon, 35400 Saint-Malo-* Directly on the beach and only a pleasant 1km stroll from the old town. The rooms are clean and many have a view of the sea from the balcony. There is limited parking and WIFI. Rooms from €65.

Vets

Clinique Veterinaire Broceliande, *Rue de Grand Jardin, 35400, Brittany. Tel: +33 2 99 81 94 51.*

Veterinaire Briocelande Dr Hakim- *58 Avenue du Miroir aux Fees, Ille-et-Vilaine, Brittany 35400. Tel: +33 2 99 81 94 51.*

Carnac

Known throughout the world for its unique rows of standing stones. The town also boasts a fantastic beach, Carnac-Plage.

Getting there
Car- Paris- 4 hrs 40, St-Malo- 2 hrs 20, Cherbourg- 3 hrs 40, Caen- 3 hrs 10, Calais- 6 hrs 10.
Rail- The nearest train station is about 9 miles away, at Auray, there are trains to here from Paris that take around 3 hrs 40 (from €30).

See & Do
The standing stones of Carnac- Arguably Brittany's greatest attraction. Three fields contain around 3,000 of the megaliths, dating from 4000 BC. The stones were erected on the spot where they were dug, hence the differing sizes. Nobody knows why they were erected but it is speculated that they had some sort of religious significance.
Carnac-Plage has five sheltered sandy beaches, which are backed by attractive 19th-century villas and pine trees. The beach at Plouharnel allows dogs.

Sleep
The Best Western Plus Celtique Hotel & Spa, *17 Ave de Kermario Cd, 82 Avenue des Druides, 56340 Carnac-* A comfortable hotel with a heated swimming pool, steam room and wellness centre. Rooms are a little

cramped but it's only 50 meters from the beach (from €90).

Hotel Le Churchill, *70 Boulevard de la Plage, 56340 Carnac*- Directly in front of the beach with plenty of free parking. It's a pleasant 15 minute walk to the centre. The rooms are good looking and clean, some have balconies and a sea view (from €80).

Vets
Daudin Anne, *9 Avenue du Rahic, 56340 Carnac, France.* Tel: +33 2 97 52 19 33.

The Gulf of Morbihan

In the temperate south of Brittany, the Gulf of Morbihan is a real gem and has been described as one of the most beautiful bays in the world. There are ancient stones in **Locmariaquer**, a walled town at **Vannes** and around 40 islands (depending on the tide). Most of the islands are privately owned but two of the largest ones are accessible, and dogs are allowed on both.

Getting there
Car- Paris- 4 hrs 20, St-Malo- 2 hrs, Cherbourg- 3 hrs 20, Caen- 2 hrs 50, Calais- 6 hrs, Roscoff- 2 hrs 30.
Rail- Vannes has a train station, there are trains from Paris that take around 3 hrs 40 (from €25), from here you can catch boats to the islands.

See & Do
Boat trips to the Islands- There are around 42 islands depending on the tides. The two largest, **Île aux Moines** and **Île d'Arz**, are favourite tourist destinations in summer. Île aux Moines is cross shaped and has plenty of scenic walks while Arz has lovely creeks and coves to enjoy a dip. Boats for both of these depart from **Vannes**.
Locmariaquer- Would be an unremarkable village were it not for its three Neolithic monuments. All three are impressive but **Le Grand Menhir**, now on the ground in four pieces, is the largest stone ever erected by Neolithic man.
Vannes- Strolling around the walled town's narrow, cobbled streets and half timbered houses is a delight.

There are medieval gates and an attractive marina. Here you'll also find boats to the islands.

Sleep

Mercure Vannes Le Port, *19 Rue Daniel Gilard | Le Parc du Golfe, 56000 Vannes-* A good hotel as long as you don't mind a good walk to the centre. It's more like 20-25 minutes than the 10 minutes stated on their website. The rooms are comfortable and parking is free. Rooms from €60.

ibis styles Vannes Gare Centre, *26 Place de la gare, 56000 Vannes-* Conveniently located next to the train station and a short walk into town. Rooms are modern and clean though definitely on the small side. Breakfast is included in the price and there is a communal PC in the lobby if you need it. Rooms from €70.

Vets

Clinique vétérinaire Roosevelt, *26 Avenue du Président Franklin Roosevelt 56000 Vannes. Tel: +33 2 97 63 09 32.*

Clinique Vétérinaire Docteur Marquet Eric, *30 Ter Avenue de la Marne 56000 Vannes.*

Worth visiting

One of the most enduring images of Brittany is of a cottage built between two massive boulders. The house is just over a mile away from **Plougrescant** in Eastern Brittany. You can't access the cottage but it makes an amazing view from across the small bay. The coast nearby has excellent walks (2 hrs west of St-Malo by car).

Rennes- Brittany's administrative capital is worth a visit. Wander round the medieval streets of the old town and admire the impressive parliament building or relax in the Thabor gardens .

Dinan- One of the most attractive and best preserved small towns in Brittany. Ramparts, half-timbered houses, an attractive port and cobbled streets make it well worth a day trip.

St-Goustan Once a very busy port, St-Goustan is now a popular site in Morbihan, full of half-timbered houses and a port.

Île de Batz (pronounced 'ba') is a hidden gem that is worth seeking out. The main attraction is its exotic garden but there are also some lovely beaches, the ruins of an 11th Century chapel, leisurely walks and a lighthouse. It's a 15-minute boat ride from Roscoff (€8.50), dogs are welcome aboard at no charge.

The **Côte d'Émeraude (Emerald Coast)**- Stretching from Cancale to Cap Frehel this lovely stretch of coast is dotted with traditional family seaside resorts, rocky headlands and safe sandy beaches. It becomes wilder towards Cap Frehel, after which the rocks start to turn a shade of pink. There are dog friendly sections of beaches on the map below.

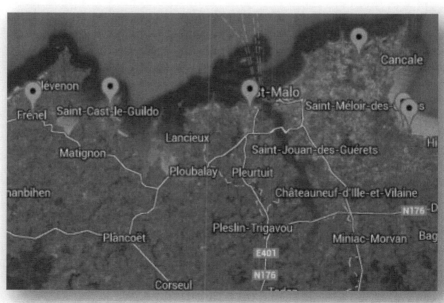

Champagne

Reims

Reims was pretty much flattened in the First World War and consequently feels a little modern. The main reason to visit is the miles upon miles of Champagne caves, though you are unlikely to be allowed in with a dog to most of them.

Getting there
Car- Paris (1 hr 30), St-Malo (5 hrs), Calais (2 hrs 30), Dieppe (3 hrs), Le Havre (3 hrs 15), Caen (3 hrs 40).
Train- Paris (50 mins, from €16).

See & Do
There is an **old centre**, with an impressive Gothic cathedral and an ancient **Roman triumphal arch**. The arch dates back to the third century BC and stands an impressive 13 metres high and 32 metres wide. The cathedral was competed in 1311 and has been the scene of coronations for French kings. There are stone effigies of France's 56 kings at the Gallery of Kings on the western façade.
Abbaye St-Remi- Reims' other historical attraction has conserved the relics of Saint Remi since 1099. Remi was the Bishop of Reims, who converted Clovis, King of the Franks, to Christianity in AD496.

Sleep

Holiday Inn Reims Centre, *46 Rue Buitrette, 51100 Reims-* A clean, modern chain hotel with large rooms and excellent facilities. Centrally located and relatively easy to find (from €100).

Grand Hotel des Templiers, *22 rue des Templiers, 51100 Reims-* A boutique hotel with lovely rooms and charming decor, which is anything but neutral. The marble bathrooms have robes and nice accessories. It's the polar opposite of a chain hotel (from €100).

Campanile Hotel Reims, *37 boulevard Paul Doumer, 51100 Reims-* A cheap, functional hotel that's clean and reasonably well placed. It's a 5-10 minute walk to the cathedral and other attractions and also near the canal for nice walks. There is a car park but it is rather expensive at €10 a day (rooms from €60).

Vets

Clinical Veterinary Jean Jaurès, *51 Avenue Jean Jaurès 51100 Reims. Tel: +33 3 26 88 79 20.*

Nicolas Bouillon, *68 Boulevard Saint-Marceaux, 51100 Reims. Tel: +33 3 26 91 11 32*

Troyes

The ancient capital of the Champagne region and probably the town in Champagne of most interest to dog owners. In fact Troyes even has its own tourism booklet dedicated to pet owners. The leaflet contains a list of parks and gardens that dogs can be exercised in, animal services, pet friendly hotels and pet friendly restaurants.

Getting there
Car- Paris (1 hr 55), St-Malo (5 hrs), Calais (3 hrs 30), Dieppe (3 hrs 45), Le Havre (3 hrs 45), Caen (4 hrs) Reims (1 hr 20).
Train- Paris -1 hr 25 (€15). Unfortunately there are no direct services from **Reims** to **Troyes.**

See & Do
Troyes is filled with marvellous churches such as the high-naved **St-Pantaléon,** with its numerous 16th century statues, or **St-Jean-au-Marché**, the church where Henry V of England married Catherine of France.
Troyes also has some of the best examples of half timbered **medieval houses** in all of Europe. Strolling along the cobbled streets is a very pleasant way to spend the day.
There are numerous nice **parks and squares**. Many of the parks have dog toilets, known as **caninsites**, which are regularly raked and cleaned by the local authorities.
The Seine river runs through the city, dividing the downtown area roughly in two, and makes for a pleasant stroll.

Sleep

Clarion Collection Hotel Saint Jean, *51 Rue Paillot de Montabert, 10000, Troyes-* A grand old hotel with spacious rooms smack in the middle of Troyes in a pedestrian area. Because of the location you can't drive direct to the hotel direct. The car park has its own sat nav location, so take heed of the instructions on your booking. It's then easy to walk to the hotel (rooms from €80).

ibis Styles Troyes Centre, *Rue Camille Claudel, 10000 Troyes-* Easily accessed with parking nearby (€10). It's modern, comfortable and clean with lively decor. The centre of the city is easily reached on foot in about ten minutes (rooms from €80). There is an ibis Budget across the road where rooms are more basic but around 30% cheaper.

Vets

Egas Pierre, *22 Rue Jaillant Deschainets, 10000 Troyes, France. Tel: 33 3 25 73 14 93.*

Alain Quiqueré, *20 Quai de Dampierre, 10000 Troyes. Tel: 33 3 25 73 17 97.*

Alsace and Lorraine

Strasbourg

The capital of Alsace and most famous (or infamous) as the host a number of important European institutions, including the European Parliament. It also boasts a beautiful historical centre- the Grande Île- which was the first to be classified as a World Heritage Site by UNESCO.

Getting there
Train- Paris- 2 hrs 20 mins (€40), Metz 1 hr 20 (€25), Nancy 1 hr 25 (€25), Dijon 2 hrs (€27).
Car- Paris- 4 hrs 20, Dijon- 3 hrs 10, Calais- 5 hrs 30.

See & Do
Strasbourg centre is easily negotiated on foot, as it is concentrated on a small island encircled by the River Ill and a canal. The spire of the pink cathedral is also visible throughout the city, so it's easy to find your bearings if you're lost. Place Gutenberg to the south is the city's main square. About a ten-minute walk west, on the tip of the island, is picturesque La Petite France, where timber-framed houses and canals hark back to the city's medieval trades of tanning and dyeing.
Cathederal de Notre Dame- The 142 metre tower throws itself upward from the cobbled streets and is undeniably Strasbourg's highlight. It is the highest in France and for 400 years was the highest in all Christen-

dom. If you travel in a group of more than one be sure to visit the nave and look out for the small sleeping dog carved into the stone pulpit. The carving depicts the dog of a clergyman who would bring his dog along to his notoriously lengthy sermons, which his dog would sleep through.

Palais des Rohan- An amazing baroque building that houses three fantastic museums, including rooms that Marie Antoinette stayed in.

L'Opera- Another beautiful baroque building and home to the city's famous opera company L'Opera National du Rhin.

Petite France is the name given to the small area between the rivers, just south of the Grande Île. It is home to some of Strasbourg's prettiest and most photogenic streets and buildings, with half timbered townhouses leaning out over the narrow cobbled streets. The old town also houses a beautiful classical park with a small zoo featuring birds and a few other animals. The park is accessible to dogs on a leash.

European district buildings, including: Council of Europe's seat (**Le Palais de l'Europe**) (1977), built by Henry Bernard; **European Court of Human Rights** (1995), built by Richard Rogers; **European Parliament** (1999), built by Architecture Studio.

Sleep
Hotel Villa d'Est, 12 Rue Jacques Kable, 67000 Strasbourg- *Although a 10-15 minute walk outside the Grande*

Ile, this hotel makes up for it by having well decorated and comfortable rooms. Breakfast is on the expensive side but cafes and patisseries are abundant on the main island so head that way for cheaper eats (rooms from €80).

Comfort Hotel Strasbourg Ouest, *14, Rue des Corroyeurs, 67200 Strasbourg-* Clean but small rooms in a decent location, as you can walk into the centre along the river, which takes about 20 minutes. Free WIFI and car park (rooms from €45).

Best Western Hotel De France, *20 Rue Du Jeu Des Enfants, 67000 Strasbourg-* In the middle of the historical centre and 10 minutes walk to La Petit France. The rooms are modern and with a decent sized bathroom (from €80).

Vets

Scanner veterinary des Halles, *28 Rue du Faubourg de Saverne, 67000 Strasbourg. Tel: +33 3 88 32 33 32.*

Clinical Veterinarian Dr. Poirier, *13 Rue de Wissembourg, 67000 Strasbourg. Tel: +33 3 88 32 69 14.*

BCMA VETERINARY, *3 Way Brass, 67200 Strasbourg. Tel: +33 3 88 29 10 56.*

Metz

The city has origins stretching further back than Roman times and it was an independent republic until 1552. Unfortunately it has since endured much hand-changing between Germany and France. Consequently it has a confusing ambiance and it's easy to forget which country you are in.

Getting there
Train-Paris- 1 hr 30 mins (€40), Strasbourg 1 hr 20 (€25), Nancy 35 mins(€10), Dijon 3 hrs (€28).
Car- Paris- 3 hrs, Dijon- 2 hrs 30, Calais- 4 hrs, Strasbourg- 1 hr 35.

See & Do
Cathedrale St-Etienne- Built between 1220 and 1522, the **enormous Saint-Etienne Cathedral** has **a nave that launches itself 42 metres into the sky.** There are also an astonishing 6,500 m² of stained glass windows.
Place d'Armes- The square next to the cathedral, is notable for the four lovely buildings that surround it. They were specifically designed to show the balance between the various local powers: the cathedral, the military, the government and justice.
Opera-Théâtre- Not far from the Cathedral, is a theatre and opera house, built between 1732 and 1752 and the oldest in France.
Gardens and river walks- Metz is known to be a *garden-city*, crossed by the Moselle and the Seille rivers, with many islands in the town centre. There are

more than 470 hectare of gardens and numerous riverside paths to stroll on.

Saint-Pierre aux Nonnains church- The oldest church in France, built in 380 AD as a gymnasium for a Roman spa complex, before being converted into the chapel for a Benedictine nunnery.

Sleep

Hotel La Citadelle Metz, *5 Avenue Ney, 57000 Metz*- A beautiful old building within 5 minutes walk of the city centre. The rooms are small and fairly dark (make sure you ask for non smoking). The restaurant has a Michelin star, no less, so don't go looking for a simple snack (from €140).

ibis Metz Centre Cathedrale, *47 rue Chambiere, Quartier Pontiffroy, 57000 Metz*- A 15 minute walk from the cathedral and with a sun terrace overlooking a park and the river. You don't choose ibis for its wide open spaces but the rooms are clean, modern and cheap (from €80).

Campanile Metz Technopole, *Technopole 2000, 2 Boulevard de la Solidarite, 57070 Metz*– Pleasant enough motel style hotel. Good for a stopover but not really for more than a night or two. It's close to the motorway but has good soundproofing. The hotel suits drivers more than travellers using public transport, but two bus routes pass the hotel (rooms from €40).

Vets

Clinical Veterinary Saint Bernard, *15 Rue de Paris, 57000 Metz. Tel: +33 3 87 32 06 06.*
Clinical Veterinarian Dr. Maller, *63 Rue in the Arena, 57000 Metz. Tel: +33 3 87 55 10 22.*

Cabayot Christian, *22 Rue Jean Burger, 57070 Saint-Julien-lès-Metz. Tel: +33 3 87 36 19 19.*

Worth visiting

Verdun- 70km west of Metz and of no particular interest in itself other than its role in the First World War. One of the most horrific battle of the whole war took place to the north of Verdun between 1916 and 1918, with hundreds of thousands dying on both sides in the battle and the entire area being completely flattened. You'll need a car to visit the area as the tour companies will not accept dogs. The main sights are strewn along the D913 and D112.

The **Alsace Wine Route** winds its way from north to south, for more than a hundred miles along the eastern foothills of the Vosges. You'll pass plenty of undulating hills and quaint medieval towns and villages, characterised by half-timbered houses, cobbled streets and ruined castles.

Nancy is renowned for its grand centre, with three plazas: **Place de la Carriere**, **Place d'Alliance** and **Place Stanislas** forming a single entry on the UNESCO World Heritage list. There are lots of parks and a very picturesque 14th century city gate, **La Porte de la Craffe**, with twin towers that give it the look of a fairy tale castle.

Loire Valley

Blois

The Loire is undoubtedly one of the grandest rivers anywhere in Europe with a parade of castles, palaces and mansions. Indeed the entire valley is a World Heritage Site.

The magnificent château at **Blois** is the main reason for visiting the town. It was home to six kings and as such is steeped in history.

Getting there
Car- Paris (2 hrs), St-Malo (3 hrs 30), Calais (4 hrs 20), Dieppe (3 hrs 30), Le Havre (3 hrs 30), Caen (3 hrs).
Train- Blois is easily reached from Tours or Orléans by train, which are both easy to reach from Paris.

See & Do
As you'd expect from somewhere that was home to six kings the **Château de Blois** is an awe-inspiring spectacle, inside and out. Unfortunately dogs are not allowed inside at all but the Hotel de France and ibis Blois Centre Château sit at the foot of the **château with rooms from under €50 in the former and** €75 in the ibis so it might be possible to leave the dog for an hour while visiting the **château, or take turns to visit it while someone stays with the dog.**
Forêt de Blois and **Forêt de Boulogne** are woodlands close to the town. They are ideal for dog walking.

Blois makes a great base because of its **proximity to other châteaux.** From here you could walk along minor roads and woodland paths to several other **châteaux in the area.**

Sleep
Hôtel de France et de Guise, *3 rue Gallois, 41000 Blois-* Very close to Château de Blois and St. Louis Cathedral. If you're looking for smart decoration and luxury then this might not be for you but if you want a warm, friendly hotel in a great position then it offers value for money. Complimentary WIFI in public areas. Rooms from €50.

ibis Blois Centre Château, *3 rue Porte Côte, 41000 Blois-* **A good base for exploring the local** châteaux. Five minutes walk from the centre and the Château, Clean and modern rooms as you'd expect from ibis, free WIFI, parking 5-10 minutes from the hotel (rooms from €75).

Vets
Clinical Veterinary Bridge Gabriel, *67 Wilson Avenue, 41000 Blois. Tel: +33 2 54 74 33 55.*
Bayle Charlotte, *31 Quai Ulysse Besnard, 41000 Blois. Tel: +33 2 54 74 87 00.*

Tours

As the biggest town of the Loire valley Tours is an important hub for the surrounding region and the main transport link to the châteaux in the area. It also has its own sights, not least St-Gatien cathedral.

Getting there
Train- The TGV from Paris Montparnasse costs about €40 each way and takes just over 1 hr.
Car- Paris (2 hrs 15), St-Malo (3 hrs), Calais (4 hrs 40), Dieppe (3 hrs 20), Le Havre (3 hrs 10), Caen (2 hrs 30).

See & Do
Walk through the colourful **old city** which is and full of fine old buildings.
Visit the place where **Joan of Arc** had her armour made, right in the heart of Tours.
Visit **Cathédrale St. Gatien,** a truly amazing sight with its twin towers, buttresses and gargoyles.
Les Prébendes a lovely park with pathways, flowerbeds and a small stream. Dogs allowed.

Sleep
Domaine de la Tortiniere, *10 Route de Ballan Mire, 37250 Tours*- If you're in the Loire Valley to see châteaux then you might as well stay in one. This imposing château is in a superb setting, with fabulous views across the grounds and down towards the river. Did I mention the history? The local French surrender was taken in the drawing room of this building in the

Franco-Prussian War. Some rooms are small-ish but all are comfortable and very charming. You'll need a car to get here as it's about 7 miles from Tours. Rooms from €110.

Adagio Access Tours, *41 Rue Edouard Vaillant, 37000 Tours*- In the heart of Tours' business district, between the TGV train station and the Palais des Congrès. Spacious apartments with kitchens, ranging from 2-person studios to 2-room apartments for 4 people, and almost all with a balcony or terrace. The city centre is a few minutes' walk away, with buses and trams close by. Direct access to the A10 highway (rooms from €60).

Best Western L'Artist Hotel, *13-15 Rue Frederic Joliot Curie, 37000 Tours*- Very convenient for the train station (150 metres) and centre of town. The rooms aren't huge but are clean and comfortable. Parking is available but can be a challenge in a large car. Rooms from €70.

Vets
Clinical Veterinary Doctors Guiraud and Hardy SCP, *5 Place de la Victoire, 37000 Tours. Tel: +33 2 47 38 22 22.*
Clinical Veterinary, *28 Avenue André Malraux, 37000 Tours. Tel: +33 2 47 66 71 94.*

Amboise

Final resting place of Leonardo da Vinci and the childhood home of Louis VIII, Amboise sits on the bank of the Loire, watched over by its fortified château.

Getting there
Car- Paris (2 hrs), St-Malo (3 hrs 30), Calais (4 hrs 40), Dieppe (3 hrs 50), Le Havre (3 hrs 30), Caen (2 hrs 40).
Train- Amboise is easily reached from Tours or Orléans by train, which are both easy to reach from Paris.

See & Do
Château du Clos Lucé Parc- Leonardo da Vinci's residence complete with an exhibition of his inventions. At the time of writing dogs could wander through the park on a leash but must be in the arms or in a carrier if you want to visit the house.
Château d'Amboise - Dogs are allowed in the castle provided they are kept on a leash and you can visit the royal residence provided to carry it in your arms or in a carrier.

Sleep
Le Clos d'Amboise, *27 Rue Rabelais, 37400 Amboise*- Very old and stylish house in the middle of the city. Lovely gardens and within walking distance of the château. Expensive but luxurious (from €140).

ibis Amboise hotel, *Z.I. La Boitardière, Chemin du Roy, 37400 Amboise-* A typical ibis hotel, nicely situated in green surroundings close to the Amboise forest. No lift, so if stairs are a problem ask for ground floor (from €70).

Vets
Sci Allard Cassabe Pilorge Rankowski, *11 Rue Joyeuse, 37400 Amboise. Tel: +33 2 47 57 00 38.*
Clinical Veterinary Allard Fleury Pilorge and Rankowski
12 Avenue de Tours, 37400 Amboise. Tel: +33 2 47 57 00 38.

Worth visiting

The gardens at **Château de Villandry** are a highlight of the region and dogs are welcome on a leash. Even in winter, there is almost always something to see here, as the entire area is replanted twice a year.

Domaine du Château de Chaumont- Dogs are allowed in the garden and castle park. The castle is situated 40 meters above the river with spectacular views of the valley as well as the turreted castle and gardens themselves.

Orléans Forest is a wilderness criss-crossed by thousands of kilometres of forest roads, many a legacy of royal hunts. With 35,000 hectares, it is the biggest state-owned forest in France with three species of eagle making their home there.

Burgundy and Rhône-Alpes

Dijon

Dijon is probably most famous for its mustard, which is still produced locally and available to buy in a hundred different forms throughout the city. Dijon is also one of the most beautiful cities in France, with a centre filled with medieval and Renaissance buildings that were largely spared during the bombing in World War Two.

Getting there
Car-Paris-3 hrs, Calais 5 hrs.
Train- The TGV will whisk you from Paris in just over an hour and a half. There is also a special return ticket on the TER from Paris which takes 3 hours but costs only €18, and lets you spend 24 hours in Dijon. The train departs from Paris-Bercy on Saturdays at 3.20 pm, arriving in Dijon at 6.14 pm, the return departs from Dijon on Sundays at 7:46 p.m., arriving in Paris-Bercy at 10:44 p.m. You can only buy this at the stations in Paris Bercy and Paris Gare de Lyon.

See & Do
Eglise Notre-Dame- A towering 13th century church with three tiers of leering gargoyles. The owl, or La Chouette, carved onto the side is Dijon's icon. Legend claims it will grant you any wish when you touch it with your left hand.
Place François Rude is a central square with beautiful

traditional houses, a fountain and a lot of cafés and bars.

The Ducal Palace (*Palais Ducal*) is a beautiful building with a neoclassical facade and a museum containing priceless treasures and wonderful art that was the property of the Dukes of Burgundy.

The cathedral (Cathédrale Sainte-Bénigne) was built over the tomb of St Benignus in the 14th century. Many of Burgundy's greatest citizens are buried within the crypt.

The Jardin Darcy is a beautiful landscaped garden with balustrades, pools, waterfalls and a Japanese pagoda. There is even a polar bear overlooking the entrance, don't worry it's only a statue. Dogs are welcome as long as they are on a leash.

Sleep
Kyriad Prestige Dijon Centre, *22 Av du Marechal Foch,*

21000 Dijon- In the heart of Dijon, right outside the Dijon Ville TGV station. This can be problematic if the sound of trains and trams bothers you. Rooms are clean, stylish and a good size. Complimentary WIFI, satellite TV and indoor pool. Rooms from €80.

Hotel Du Palais, *23 Rue Du Palais, 21000 Dijon*- Great location, about 2 minutes walk to the centre, parking on the street outside the hotel is very cheap. Beds are comfortable, but some are very small. There is also no lift, but the rooms are very cheap (from €60).

The ibis Dijon Gare, *15a Avenue Albert 1er, 21000 Dijon* – Convenient for drivers and rail alike, located 300 m from the train station and with free parking. The hotel is close to Dijon's historic city centre. Rooms are large enough and spotlessly clean (from €75).

Vets

Clinical Veterinary Republic, *7 Bis Rue Parmentier, 21000 Dijon. Tel: +33 3 80 74 46 46.*

Dr. Labourdette, *47 Avenue Aristide Briand, 21000 Dijon. Tel: +33 3 80 71 40 94.*

Adrien Andrianoel, *56 Avenue of Flag, 21000 Dijon. Tel: +33 3 80 71 44 10.*

Lyon

Founded by the Romans and with many preserved historical areas, Lyon is France's third largest city and its gastronomic capital. Lyon is also full of parks and is a gateway to the Alps with Grenoble, Chamberry, Annecy and Geneva all around an hour away.

Getting there
Car- Calais-6 hrs 30, Paris 4 hrs 10.
Train- There are three train stations in Lyon: Perrache, Part-Dieu and Saint-Exupéry (the latter of which is outside the city and serves the airport). TGVs to and from Paris serve both Perrache and Part-Dieu stations; other TGVs generally serve only Part-Dieu. Ouigo, the budget TGV service serves Part-Dieu and Saint-Exupéry.
From Paris the TGV train takes around 2 hrs. Fares from Marne la Vallee to Saint-Exupéry with Ouigo are as little as 10€ and take less than two hours.
Note on getting around
At the time of writing only guide dogs and small dogs in bags were allowed on the local Lyon Metro service. There is a scheme for residents whereby they can pass a test and obtain a pass for their dog but this isn't practical for tourists. Consequently travellers might want to choose a hotel close to the main areas of interest.

See & Do
Roman theatre Fourvière- Lyon's Roman theatre is the oldest in France, built from 17 to 15 BC and expanded

during the reign of Hadrian. Ruins of three ancient Roman structures - a theater, odeum and temple - cluster together on Fourvière Hill just south of the Fourvière Basilica.

Fourvière Basilica- Dedicated to the Virgin Mary, this massive church made of white marble sits on the crown of Fourvière hill. It's a stunning church, with architectural elements from Classical and Gothic eras. Next to the basilica is a viewpoint from where you can see Mount Blanc on a clear day. There's a smaller version of the Eiffel Tower here as well. The tower is now used as a TV mast.

Vieux Lyon- Old Lyon is the second largest Renaissance area in Europe. With narrow, colourful streets dating back to the Middle Ages. Highlights include the astronomical clock in St Jean cathedral and the traboules.

Traboules- These corridors which link two streets through a building, and usually a courtyard are unique architectural masterpieces and are a must for any visit to Lyon. They can be found in Vieux Lyon and Croix-Rousse.

Parc de la Tête d'Or- France's largest, and arguably most beautiful, urban park, which is popular with dog walkers. The highlights of the park include the large greenhouses, the botanical garden, the rose garden and the recently added "African plain" in which animals wander in a natural-style environment. Dogs are allowed everywhere, including the zoo, as long as they are kept on a leash. There are also designated areas for them to romp around unleashed and make new friends.

Amphithéâtre des Trois Gaules- Documents claim this was the largest theatre in Gaul at one time, but nobody knows exactly how far it extends under the neighbouring buildings, nor what remains from the Roman era after centuries of construction. The theatre can be seen from the street but is not open to the public for safety reasons.

Sleep

Adagio Access Lyon, *14 rue Jacqueline Auriol, Angle 55 avenue Jean Mermoz, 69008 Lyon-* Close to the Maison de la Danse, this aparthotel has a range of studios and 2-room apartments all equipped with a kitchen. There is a tram stop nearby, the ring road is 2 minutes away and an undercover car park is available from €70.

Campanile Lyon Centre Gare Perrache, *17 Place Carnot, 69002 Lyon-* Centrally located in Lyon, steps from Place Carnot and minutes from Textile Museum. This hotel is within close proximity of Saint Martin d'Ainay Abbey and University of Lyon II. Complimentary WIFI in the lobby. Paid parking is located nearby. Rooms from €80.

Mama Shelter, *13 rue Domer, 69007 Lyon-* The very antithesis of a chain hotel, this quirky, ultra modern establishment is a visual delight. Some of the rooms are a little on the small side so try to contact the hotel and ask for a larger one when booking. The hotel also has regular deals with rooms from as little as €69, an absolute steal. The hotel is a 30 minute walk to the main areas of interest.

Vets

Clinical Veterinary Saxony, *142 Avenue Marechal de Saxe, 69003 Lyon. Tel: +33 4 78 60 17 59.*

Clinical Veterinary Kirchner, *71 Rue Boileau, 69006 Lyon. Tel: +33 4 78 94 03 31.*

Clinical Veterinary Lafayette Bridge, *23 Quai Général Sarrail, 69006 Lyon. Tel: +33 4 78 24 32 77.*

Annecy

The Venice of Savoie, this beautiful medieval town is criss-crossed by canals and streams running out of Lake Annecy. The lake is one of the world's purest lakes, aquamarine and perfect for swimming while surrounded by mountains.

Getting there
Car-Lyon (1 hr 30),Paris (5 hrs), Calais (7 hrs 30)
Train- Paris- 4 hrs (€50) or Lyon- 2 hrs (€25).

See & Do
Old town- The 17th century old town is full of pastille coloured buildings, strolling around them provides dozens of photo opportunities.

Palais d'Isle- A former palace-turned-prison, sits on an island between the canals.

Château d'Annecy- A 13th to 16th century castle situated on a hill overlooking the city and the surroundings, worth a stroll to the top.

Swim, sail or walk around the lake-There are several parks lining the waterfront, with opportunities for your dog to swim near the harbour near the town centre as well as quieter sections of the lake. The average water temperature in July is a reasonable 22 degrees so it's possible to swim in the crystal clear waters together. Your best bet is to drive/walk along the lake until you find an area where there is no official looking signs (to say that it is a recognised beach) and enjoy your own area.

Sleep

Hotel du Palais de l'Isle, *13 rue Perriere, 74000 Annecy-* Right in the middle of the old town, about 10 minutes walk to the train and bus stations. Some rooms have balconies overlooking the canal, the old prison and people dining in the cafes below. Others are a tad small but all are clean and comfortable. Rooms from €100.

Splendid Hotel, *4 quai Eustache Chappuis, 74000 Annecy-* Very well located hotel with comfortable beds and modern decor. The rooms are spacious enough and some have mountain views. Parking is close by but not free. Rooms from €89.

ibis Annecy Centre Vieille Ville, *12 rue de la Gare | Ilôt de la Manufacture, 74000 Annecy-* Typical ibis rooms, clean and comfortable though not exactly huge. The hotel has a great location, next to the canal in the old town and within walking distance of the lake and castle. Rooms from €80.

Vets

Coudert Laurence, *7 Rue Louis Revon, 74000 Annecy, Tel: +33 4 50 52 75 44.*
Clinical Veterinary Lafayette, *9 Rue Thomas Ruphy, 74000 Annecy. Tel: +33 4 50 23 36 95.*

Chamonix

A world famous resort that sits under the Mont Blanc massif. Here you'll find amazing scenery and some of the world's most spectacular cable car rides.

Getting there
Car- Lyon (2 hrs 15), Paris (5 hrs 30), Calais (7 hrs 45).
Train-Lyon- 4 hrs (€45, with 2 changes) Paris- 5 hrs 40 (€45).
Tip-There are two alternative ways of getting there via train. The first is to catch a train to Geneva Airport from Paris (3 hrs) then a shuttle to Chamonix (45 minutes). The second is to catch the Intercities Night Train (bookable on SNCF's website). The train leaves Paris at 23:12 and arrives in Saint Gervais Les Bains at 08:45, where you change train and arrive at Chamonix at 09:50. The train has sleeping compartments so is an interesting alternative to travelling by day.

See & Do
The Alps- Chamonix has some of the highest and most spectacular cable cars in the world. Unfortunately dogs are not allowed on **all** of them. They are however allowed on the one to **Le Brevant**, the highest peak on the western side of the valley (elevation 2500 meters), with amazing views of **Mount Blanc**. The cable car is not for the faint of heart and you'll be glad of the fogged windows. Once at the summit dogs are restricted to

certain trails below but you'll be treated to an amazing view of Mount Blanc.

There are six separate lift systems spread throughout the **Chamonix Valley**, all offering a wide variety of activities. Dogs are allowed on all of the following but may be required to wear a lead where directed: Brevent & Flegere, Domaine de la Balme, Les Grands Montets, Montenvers and Train du Mont Blanc.

Please remember that dogs can suffer from altitude sickness and that it would be irresponsible to venture to extreme altitudes.

Sleep

Mercure Chamonix Les Bossons, *59 Route blanche Vers le Nant, Les Bossons, 74400 Chamonix*- Great location if driving, 5 minutes from the Aiguille du Midi cable cars & the Mer de Glace glacier train. Large bedrooms, with stunning views of the Alps (ask for a glacier view when booking). Free outdoor car park, indoor car park & free shuttle to Chamonix when you leave. The hotel also has a fitness area, sauna, indoor swimming pool & whirlpool bath with views of Mont Blanc. Rooms from €80.

La Croix-Blanche, *81 rue Vallot, BP 135, 74404 Chamonix*- Beautifully located in central Chamonix with views of Brevent and Aiguille du Midi. Some rooms also have a terrace, there's free parking and it's also close to the centre. There is no elevator in the hotel if stairs are a problem. Rooms from €65.

Gustavia Hotel, *272 avenue Michel-Croz, 74400 Chamonix*- A good value budget hotel in a central location opposite the station and a few minutes from the Aguille du Midi. Rooms are comfortable, clean and spacious enough. The only real downside is the proximity of a bar over the road, which can get a little noisy at times. Rooms from €65.

Vets

Thomas Colson, *120 Square Hairy, 74400 Chamonix-Mont-Blanc. Tel: +33 9 65 11 43 54.*

Maillier Franck, *120 Square Hairy, 74400 Chamonix-Mont-Blanc. Tel: +33 4 50 53 50 85.*

Worth a visit

Mont Blanc is Western Europe's highest peak, and is a spectacular sight. Annecy is the easiest city from which to approach the mountain if you're in a car. There are two road routes, the one east via Megève being the more scenic. The roads meet at **Le Fayet**, a village just outside St-Gervais-les-Bains. This is where the Tramway du Mont Blanc begins its 75-minute journey to the Nid d'Aigle (2375m), a vantage point on the northwest slope (€27.40 return, dogs allowed on a leash).

If you're using rail there is a train from **Annecy** to **St-Gervais-les-Bains-Le Fayet** that takes approximately 1 hr 30 and costs €15. There is also a night service from Paris to **St-Gervais-les-Bains** arriving at 08:45.

Grenoble has three mountain ranges right on its doorstep and as such is an ideal destination for travellers who love the outdoors. In fact whichever way you look you'll be treated to mountain views. It's also a vibrant student city with plenty to see and do. There are lovely parks, fantastic vantage points, old fortifications and medieval buildings. There is a train from Paris that takes about three hours.

Lac du Bourget is France's biggest natural lake. 12 miles long and over 2 miles wide it is a place of outstanding natural beauty and a wildlife reserve. The largest town on the shore is Aix-les-Bains, while Chambéry lies about 6 miles south of the lake. Aix-les-Bains can be reached directly by train from Paris (3 hrs) for as little as €30. It's a 30 minute drive from Annecy or 1 hr 15 from Lyon.

Atlantic Coast

La Rochelle

La Rochelle has one of the most photographed harbours on France's Atlantic coast. The colourful hub of a town is packed with history, heritage, tempting boutiques and cosy restaurants.

Getting there
Car- St-Malo-3 hrs 30, Paris 4 hrs 20, 4 hrs 10, Cherbourg and Le Havre 5 hrs.
Train-Paris 3 hrs 15 (€54)

See & Do
The Old Port ("Vieux Port")- The most picturesque part of La Rochelle. Most of the buildings are hundreds of years old. The narrow streets and pale stone buildings give the Old Port a distinctly Mediterranean feel. Three towers dating back to medieval times stand guard over the port.
Port des Minimes- An enormous port crammed with pleasure boats of all sizes. There is a beach next to the port.
The **city's centre's** renaissance heritage is evident in the vaulted stone arcades, turrets and timber-framed houses of the historic centre, which was pedestrian-ised, along with the waterfront, in the 1970s

Ile de Ré- Located across a toll bridge from La Rochelle, beautiful Ile de Ré has long sandy beaches, secluded coves, designer boutiques and high end hotels/restaurants. Ars-en-Ré on the western end of the island has several beaches that allow dogs, while many patrolled beaches on the island allow dogs before 9am and after 8pm.

Sleep
ibis La Rochelle Centre Historique, *1 ter rue Fleuriau, 17000, La Rochelle-* In the heart of the city centre between the indoor market and shopping streets, 5 minutes from the old harbour and its restaurants. WIFI and a 24-hour bar and snack service. A CCTV-monitored paying public car park is located 2 minutes away. Rooms from €69.

Kyriad La Rochelle Centre, *51 rue de Perigny, 17000 La Rochelle-* Located on a business park about 10 minutes walk from the rail station and centre of town. Rooms are very clean, bright looking and a decent size with tea and coffee facilities. Rooms from €50.

Best Western Masqhotel, *17 Rue de l'Ouvrage a Corne, 17000 La Rochelle-* Just round the corner from the train station and 10 mins walk from the old port. Very personable, helpful reception staff and super clean, comfy and spacious rooms. Highly recommended, from €80.

Vets
Practice Veterinary Market, *28 Rue Thiers, 17000 La Rochelle. Tel: +33 5 46 07 20 95.*

Clinical Veterinary Saint-Roch, *18 Rue de Dompierre, 17000 La Rochelle. Tel: +33 5 46 27 16 02.*

Marais Poitevin

A beautiful maze of waterways that turn green with duckweed in the warmer months, the canals, streams and marshes cover around 800km and are dubbed Green Venice.

Getting there

Car- You can access the eastern part of the marsh from the "capital" of the region, **Coulon,** 4 hrs from Paris, 3 hrs 10 from St-Malo and 45 minutes from La Rochelle. You can also reach the lovely village of **Arçais**, with its 19th century **château**, from Paris, St-Malo and La Rochelle in a similar time.

Rail- Getting to **Arçais** without a car can be painful. But **Coulon** is only 11km from **Niort** where there are plenty of hotels and regular trains run from La Rochelle (45 minutes-€14) and Paris (2 hrs 30-from €20).

See & Do

The entire region is a haven for birdlife that you can explore by boat, bike or on foot. In many ways it is a warmer, and more dog friendly, version of the Norfolk Broads. Tourist offices stock a free guide called MARAIS POITEVIN: CARTE DÉCOUVERTE. Dogs are allowed in most areas of the national park including on many of the boats.

Sleep

ibis Niort, 260 *Avenue de la Rochelle, 79000 Niort,-* Located six miles from the Marais Poitevin and a short

---

drive from Niort. Easily accessible in a car from the A10 and A83 highways, but not really suitable if you're using trains. Standard ibis rooms, clean and comfortable, from €70.

ibis Styles Niort Centre Grand Hotel, *32-24 Avenue de Paris, 79000 Niort*- Right in the heart of things and about a ten minute walk from the train station. The rooms are modern, clean and very comfortable. Breakfast is included and is very good. Rooms from €80.

Best Western Hotel de la Breche, *9 Avenue Bujault Place de la Breche, 79000 Niort*- Very clean and modern hotel, located smack in the middle of the city centre overlooking the newly renovated Place de la Brèche. Rooms are of varying sizes so ask for a larger room when booking. Only a short walk from the train station and with parking available using a validation system. Rooms from €95.

Vets

Clinical Veterinary Vanderbecken Marc Cécile SCP, *21 Path Gayolles, 79000 Niort. Tel: +33 5 49 33 00 06.*
Clinical Veterinary Batiot Stas Mane Fraysse, *19 Chemin de Pierre, 79000 Niort. Tel: +33 5 49 73 48 61.*

Biarritz

Biarritz lies on the Bay of Biscay, on the Atlantic coast, in south-western France, 11 miles from the border with Spain. Until the 1960's Biarritz was something of a playground for the rich and famous, it is now a surf mecca and in high summer you'll be lucky to find any space in the water.

Getting there
Sail- If you are travelling this far southwest in France it might be worth considering the ferry from Portsmouth to Bilbao in Spain. Brittany Ferries run a service that has dog friendly cabins. There is an exercise area where they can meet new friends and Biarritz is only a 1 hr 40 journey once you get there! What's more, you can visit the famous towns of San Sebastian, Bilbao and Pamplona as well. The journey takes 20 hrs but your dog stays with you and the cost (from £600 return) is offset by the money you will save on petrol and road tolls.

Car- Paris (7 hrs 10), St-Malo (6 hrs 50), La Rochelle (3 hrs 45). Parking is near impossible at any time of the year, so park out of town and use the free shuttle (NAVETTE) service.

Train- From Paris the TGV takes approximately 5 hrs. Another option is to take the Lunea night train that leaves Paris everyday at 22:12 and arrives at Biarritz at 08:18. The train costs as little as £63 each way, though you might want to pay a little extra for a bed in a couchette (and if you're travelling as part of a group of four a couchette can be reserved for your sole purpose). The cost is little more than a night in a hotel and you will wake up in your destination. Dogs weighing more than six kilos travel half price, while dogs less than six kilos and travelling in a container are around five euros.

See & Do
Beaches- Biarritz is predominately a beach destination with six beaches in total. Three of these are **surf beaches, Grande Plage**, near the old town and the famous casino, being the most famous. It has beautiful views and a world famous backdrop, but dogs are not allowed on the sand; even so it's worth a stroll on the promenade behind to watch the surfers and beach life.

Plage Port Vieux is a petite little cove beach in the old town between the Grande Plage and Port Vieux where you wouldn't be in anyone's way with a dog out of the main season. At low tide there are rock pools ideal for little dogs to swim in.

Sleep
Radisson Blu Hotel, *1 Carrefour Helianthe, 64200 Biarritz*- Well-placed for the centre of Biarritz and the coast. Rooms are spacious and clean. There is a rooftop pool area with restaurant and snack bar, though we took it in turns rather than taking our dog up there. Rooms from €110.

Hotel Campanile Biarritz, *Boulevard Marcel Dassault, Rn10 Rond-point du Mousse, 64200 Biarritz*- Typical Campanile motel situated two miles from the city centre but close to the train station (which is also out of town). Complimentary WIFI cable TV, free parking with a bus running to the city from nearby. Rooms from €65.

Vets

Veterinary Clinic Beaurivage, *10 Avenue Beau Rivage, 64200 Biarritz Tel: 05 59 23 28 17.*

Arcangela Combelles PCS Vets, *27 Avenue du President John Fitzgerald Kennedy, 64200 Biarritz. Tel: +33 5 59 41 14 57.*

Katrin Scheil, *18 Rue Océan 64200 Biarritz. Tel: +33 6 73 01 24 48.*

Worth a visit

The city of **Bordeaux,** a fusion of neoclassical architecture and modern design, towers above the west bank of the River Garonne. It makes an excellent hub for exploring the surrounding region, with trains from Paris taking around three hours, it is within striking distance of lakes, sand dunes and the beaches of the **Côte d'Argent**. It also has its own charms with its striking cathedral, roman ruins and parks aplenty.

Île d'Oléron- Joined to the mainland by a bridge close to La Rochelle, the island has quaint villages, pine forests and beaches. The beach at St Pierre allows dogs before 9am and after 8pm in high summer (all day before 15th June and after 15th September), while many other beaches allow dogs outside of the peak months of July and August.

Côte d'Argent is the longest, straightest and sandiest stretch of coast in Europe. It is also backed by the largest forest in Western Europe. This makes it a perfect place to holiday with your dog, **Arcachon** and upmarket **Cap Ferrat** make particularly good bases.

Dune du Pilat- Is the tallest sand dune in Europe. 60 km from Bordeaux the dune measures 2.7km in length, 500m in width and 110 meters in height. Buses leave from the GARE SNCF in Arcachon hourly in July and August, with between two and five buses a day in other months. Dogs are allowed on the dune but not the beach below it.

Saintes- A wonderful abbey with an eleventh-century tower and one of the finest amphitheatres in France make **Saintes well worth a day trip from Bordeaux (1hr 15) or La Rochelle (1hr).**

Languedoc-Roussillion

Carcassonne

A medieval fortress settlement with more than two thousand years of history. With over 3 km of walls and 52 towers, it resembles a fairy tale fortress. *Robin Hood: Prince of Thieves* was partly shot here.

Getting there
Car- Paris (7 hrs), Marseille (2 hrs 50), Bordeaux (3 hrs), Montpellier (1 hr 30).
Train- If you or your dog can handle such a long train journey there is an Intercities train direct from Paris that takes around 7 hrs 30 but costs as little as €20. Alternately you could catch a TGV to nearby Narbonne (4 hrs 30, from €50) and then catch a local train to Carcassonne. Finally the La Lunea night train leaves from Paris every night and arrives in Carcassonne at 05:30 the next morning. Sleeping cabins must be pre-booked for your sole use if you wish to take your dog on board.

See & Do
People come to Carcassonne to see the walled and turreted fortress of the **Cité**. The medieval village with its narrow, twisting alleys give a hint of how life must have been in medieval times. Admission to these streets is free and dogs are welcome (indeed people live here). However, to see the inner fortress of the Château

Comtal and walk the walls, you'll have to join a **guided tour and dogs are not allowed.**

The city is beautifully illuminated after dark so if you get the chance try to stay over for at least one night to marvel at the sight.

The beautiful **church of St-Nazaire**, towards the southern corner of the Cité at the end of rue St-Louis. It's rose windows have some of the loveliest stained glass in the region.

Nearly 3 million tourists visit the Cité of Carcassonne every year so it can get very busy in this little town. Peak season is from June to August, if you can avoid these months do so.

Sleep

ibis Carcassonne Centre, *5 square Gambetta, 11000 Carcassonne-* Standard ibis hotel perfect for a one night stay to visit the Cité. Situated in the new town, ten minute walk from the Cité and the train station with cheap parking nearby (rooms from €70).

Mercure Carcassonne Porte de la Cite, *18 rue Camille Saint-Saens, 11000 Carcassonne-* Tucked away in a quiet street just past the main car parks for La Cite, around 2 miles from the train station. It's a pleasant, uphill stroll to the Medieval city. Rooms are large with, comfortable and clean with all the amenities you'll need. Rooms from €75.

Espace Cite, *132 Rue Trivalle, 11000 Carcassonne-* A fantastically priced hotel situated very close to the Cité. Good free car parking and small but comfortable rooms that are fine for an overnight stay as long as you don't have a huge dog. Rooms from €60.

Vets

Clinical Veterinary Pont d'Artigues, *2 Rue Pascal, 11000 Carcassonne. Tel: +33 4 68 47 93 02.*

Mondo Patrick, *173 Avenue du Président Franklin Roosevelt 11000 Carcassonne. Tel: +33 4 68 25 42 36.*

Stephane Sahun, *3 Rue des purslane, 11000 Carcassonne. Tel: +33 4 68 47 10 24.*

Côte Vermeille

A lovely stretch of coast stretching from Argelès-sur-Mer to the border of Spain's Costa Brava.

Getting there
Car- Paris 8 hrs, Marseille 3 hr 30, Montpellier 2 hrs.
Train- The best way to reach the Côte Vermeille is via Montpellier, Nimes or Perpignan. Montpellier is 3 hrs 30 from Paris, then 2 hours from Argelès-sur-Mer. Nimes is 3 hrs from Paris then 2 hrs 30 from Argelès-sur-Mer. Perpignan is 5 hours from Paris then 20 minutes from Argelès-sur-Mer.
Train & Car- A great way to discover the coast and the surrounding area is to take a Ouigo or IDTGV train to Nimes or Montpellier and then hire a car from one of the major companies, all of whom have offices in the respective train stations. Argelès-sur-Mer is a pleasant 2 hour drive from Montpellier and it's possible to take side trips to Carcassonne or the beaches of Béziers and Narbonne along the way.

See & Do
Argelès-sur-Mer- is a magnet for campers, with numerous upscale, four-star campgrounds, most featuring pools, on-site restaurants, bars and shops. The dog friendly areas are at the extreme ends of the beach so a car is preferable. Both beaches are very clean and the water is pristine. Behind the town sit the Pyrenees, indeed the town's slogan is "In the Mediterannean, the Pyrénées have a beach."

Collioure- a small town, with ochre rooftops and a castle at the edge of the shore. So picturesque is the town that it sparked a new art movement known as Fauvism, which attracted artists like Picasso to the area. They hung out at the bar of the Hôtel-Restaurant les Templiers, which doubles as an art museum now, but is still a dog friendly hotel as well. Dogs are allowed on the north section of beach.

Banyuls-sur-Mer- a village with numerous wineries perched behind it. The narrow Allées Maillol are where local artists ply their craft. It is worth visiting just for the splendid panoramic view of village, sea and mountains. It's also the last port before Spain and a good stopping off point if you want to enjoy the spectacular coastal drive across the border to Port Bou on the Costa Brava.

Drive or take the train to Spain- The drive from Banyuls-sur-Mer to Port Bou in Spain is simply stunning. The road meanders up vertiginous mountains with views of the Mediterranean below as you negotiate dozens of hairpin bends. It's not for nervous drivers who can opt for the much less dramatic train ride. The train takes 25 minutes from Argelès-sur-Mer, 20 minutes from Collioure or 12 minutes from Banyuls-sur-Mer.

Take a boat trip- Take a glass bottom boat trip, or even a boat the Costa Brava in Spain with one of the numerous operators at Port Argelès. Roussillon Croisieres operate half day and full day trips from Port Argelès to Spain, dolphin watching, local caves and many other local destinations. www.roussillon-croisieres.com.

Sleep

Hotel Le Nid, *10 rue des Grives, 66700 Argeles-sur-Mer*- A quiet hotel just steps away from the train station and with super helpful owners. The rooms aren't huge but they are clean. It's a bit of a hike from here to the dog beaches though, about 2.5 km but if you're arriving by train it's a great option. Rooms from £38.

Residence Maeva Port Argeles, *Rue Eric Tabarly, 66700 Argeles-sur-Mer*- Fantastic location right behind the port, which is really handy for bars, shops, restaurants and boat trips. It's also very close to the dog friendly section of beach. The rooms are large and have balconies overlooking the port, there are also cooking facilities which is handy if you're on a budget or don't like eating out a lot. Rooms start at around £50 a night.

Hotel-Restaurant les Templiers, *12 Quai de l'Amiraute, 66190 Collioure*- The famous hotel is just 5 minutes walk from Collioure train station, on the port and with a view of the castle. The dog section of beach is nearby so the location could not be better, especially if you're arriving by train. Visitors with a car cannot park at the hotel so will need to find street parking elsewhere. Rooms are dated and some a little small so be sure to book a larger room when booking (from £61).

Vets

Bontemps Paul, *6 Avenue du 8 Mai 1945, 66700 Argelès-sur-Mer. Tel : +33 4 68 81 04 26.*

Benhamdine Stéphanie, *3 Rue des Hérons, 66700 Argelès-sur-Mer. Tel: +33 4 68 89 20 02.*

Nimes

An easy to reach city that hosts a charming old town and some of France's best preserved Roman monuments, including a 1st century amphitheatre and a 5th century temple.

Getting there
Car- Paris 6 hrs 30, Marseille 1 hr 30, Avignon 45 mins, Montpellier 45 mins.
Train- Paris 3 hrs (from €45), Marne la Vallee (Euro-Disney) 3 hrs (from €20), regional trains run to Avignon (30 mins), Marseille (1 hr 15) and Arles (30 mins).

See & Do
Les Arene- A well preserved Roman arena that hosts bull fighting festivals in September. It was built around 100AD and currently seats 10,000. Dogs are not allowed inside unless they are carried in a bag but the exterior is a remarkable spectacle and often without a tourist in sight.
Maison Carré, a very well preserved fifth century Roman temple. Dogs are not allowed inside but the exterior is well worth a visit.
Jardin de la Fontaine, home of Nîmes' other important Roman monuments, beautiful statues, and temple of Diane, which is to the left through the main entrance. Free entrance, dogs allowed.

Sleep
Adagio Access Nimes, *5 Allee Boissy d'Anglas, Triangle de la Gare, 30000 Nimes-* Excellent location five minutes from Nimes Arena, and one minute from the train station. Carrefour Express supermarket three doors away. Spacious rooms from €55, fee for parking €8.

ibis Budget Nimes, *Avenue de la Mediterranee, 30900 Nimes-* Next to the Adagio Access and the train station. Also very close to the Arena. The rooms are small but clean with WIFI and are okay for a couple of days from €45.

Novotel Atria Nimes Centre, *5 Boulevard de Prague, 30000 Nimes-* A fantastic location, just two minutes walk from the arena and very close to the train station as well. Rooms are spacious though getting a little dated, from €90.

Vets

Boschetti Line and Chatry Dominique SCP, *51 Avenue du Général Leclerc, 30000 Nîmes. Tel: +33 4 66 29 15 30.*

Mazet Jean-Jacques and Alain Stayed SCP, *21 Avenue Franklin Roosevelt, 30000 Nîmes. Tel: +33 4 66 23 60 11.*

Froidefond Gass-Isabelle and Luc Froidefond PCS Vets, *108 Rue André Simon, 30900 Nîmes. Tel: +33 4 66 02 00 63.*

Worth a visit

Pont Du Gard- A short car or bus ride (dogs are allowed onboard) from Nimes, Pont du Gard is a very well preserved Roman aqueduct. With three tiers, thirty five arches and almost three hundred feet in length, the aqueduct is an awesome spectacle; especially when you consider its age. **Tip- Try to get there in the evening as admission to the site is charged for the museum and therefore free once the museum is closed.**

Toulouse- Is the main town in **western Languedoc** and therefore an accessible starting point for anywhere in the southwest of France. It has its own charms as well and is nicknamed the pink city after the distinctive stone used in the buildings.

Cordes- Perched on a hill 50 miles northeast of Tou-louse, is one of the region's best sights. Founded in the 13th century this **Cathar** stronghold has thirteenth and fourteenth-century houses climbing steep cobbled lanes. It looks stunning at any time, but especially so when the base of the hill is shrouded in mist.

Montpellier- A good base for the eastern **Languedoc with regular TGV trains from Paris.** Take a walk on the tree lined Esplanade but don't venture there at night when the area becomes unsafe. The nearby beach of La Grande Motte has a section for dogs.

Port Leucate is an enormous holiday development close to the border with Spain. The beach is long and very deep and there are sections where dogs are allowed. A boardwalk runs behind the beach, which is popular with roller skaters. There is plenty of parking and restaurants in the area.

Provence

Aix-en-Provence

Often referred to as Aix, this classically Provençal town, with its wonderful 17th century architecture, paved plazas and many fountains, is famous for being home to Cézanne. The city centre is compact and with narrow, car-free streets ideal for enjoying on foot.

Getting there
Car-Paris-6 hrs 40, Marseille-30 mins, Nimes-1 hr 15, Lyon -2 hrs 45.
Train- Paris-3 hrs (from €37), Marne la Vallee- 3 hrs (from €20), Lyon- 1 hr 25 (from €10), Marseille- 12 mins (from €4.50), Nimes- 45 mins (from €20).

See & Do
Aix is well known for its **fountains**, the most famous of which is on the Cours Mirabeau, where the water is drawn from a hot spring.
The **architecture** in Aix is attractive, almost stately in parts, and another good reason to visit. The tangles medieval streets with their intricate doors are a key feature, as are the bell towers.
Aix is well known as the home of **Cézanne's** later works. Indeed there is a dedicated **circuit**, marked by bronze plaques, that can be followed round town. You will see where he ate, studied, painted and drank. There is a free guide to the plaques available from the tourist office.

Parc Jourdan -A city park, covering 40,000 sq.m, reached from Rue Anatole France or Avenue Jules Ferry. There is an upper and lower part to the park with a huge double staircase connecting them. Dogs are allowed on a leash.

Dogs are also welcome in the following parks:

Parc Georges Vilers, an unfenced park in the heart of Jas de Bouffan, adjoining Avenue Saint John Perse; the gardens of **Pavillon Vendome** an 18th century mansion

Promenade de la Torse , where a path runs alongside the Torse stream, between the Cezanne Road and Route de Nice, in the eastern part of the city. At the end of the promenade sits a huge lake (2,500 sq.m), ideal for cooling off your dog on a hot summer day.

Sleep

ibis Aix en Provence, *Chemin des Infirmeries, 13100 Aix-en-Provence-* Small but clean rooms with lavender growing out front. Large car park and easy access from the highway. Pool, WIFI and restaurant. A bus runs from outside the hotel to the centre of Aix (from €65).

Hotel Novotel Aix en Provence Pont de l'Arc, *Avenue Arc De Meyran, 13100 Aix-en-Provence* -Comfortable rooms, lovely gardens, pool, great breakfast and very helpful staff. The location is good if you don't mind walking, or you can catch a bus from outside the hotel (rooms from €90).

Vets

Clinical Veterinary de la Violette, *31 Boulevard Aristide Briand, 13100 Aix-en-Provence. Tel: +33 4 42 21 19 50.*

Philippe Beauchene, *31 Boulevard Aristide Briand, 13100 Aix-en-Provence. Tel: +33 4 42 23 05 80.*
Clinical Veterinary Chartreux, *3 Boulevard Ferdinand de Lesseps, 13090 Aix-en-Provence. Tel: +33 4 42 64 60 00.*

Avignon

Avignon was the capital of the Catholic Church during the early Middle Ages when the Popes fled the corruption of Rome. The palace they built, 'Le Palais des Papes,' is the *world's largest Gothic edifice*. Its vast rooms are virtually empty nowadays but it remains a magnificent and imposing building.

Getting there
Car-Paris-6 hrs 30, Marseille- 1 hr 10, Nimes- 45 mins, Lyon 2 hrs 15.
Train- Paris- 2 hrs 40 (from €35), Marne la Vallee- 2 hrs 40 (from €15), Lyon 1 hr (from €10).
Note: Local and regional trains call at the central station, outside the walls on the southern edge of the old town. TGVs call at Avignon TGV, about 2km out of town. A regular bus links the TGV station with the central station and costs around €1.30.

See & Do
Place du Palais- The world's largest Gothic Palace, built when the popes abandoned Rome in the 14th century. The massive scale of the palace has to be seen to be believed and testifies to the immense wealth of the papacy and their need for defence.
Le Pont Saint-Benezet- A ruined bridge not far from the Palais des Papes. Legend tells that a local shepherd was inspired by angels to build a bridge. When his appeals to the town authorities did not work he picked up a massive stone and hurled it into the river, to be the

bridge's foundation. Convinced by this demonstration of divine will, the authorities had a change of heart and the bridge was then built. The shepherd boy was canonised, and has a chapel on the remaining section of the bridge. Originally, the bridge had 22 arches but following numerous floods only four remain today and the bridge ends abruptly in the middle of the river.

Sleep
Hotel Splendid, *17 rue Agricol Perdiguier, 84000 Avignon* -A charming little hotel in the historic centre, 5 minutes from the train station and TGV shuttle stop. The rooms, which are a little small, include free Wi-Fi, but the biggest asset is the location (from €90).

Adagio Access Avignon, *6 Avenue de la Gare, 84000 Avignon*- Within walking distance from TGV station in Avignon. The TGV station is out of the historic centre so you'll need to take the shuttle opposite the hotel to go the city or walk. Rooms have a small kitchen with complete utensils for cooking, free parking, WIFI in the lobby only (rooms from €50).

Best Western Hotel Du Lavarin, *1715 Chemin Du Lavarin Sud, FR-84000 Avignon*- About 10 minutes drive from historic Avignon, buses run into town. Unfortunately there are no real cafes or restaurants in the area though. Rooms are spacious and clean and with free parking. Rooms from €75.

Vets
Sorel Florence, *39 Rue Saint-Michel 84000 Avignon. Tel: +33 4 90 82 61 79.*

Discours-mombelli Christophe, *6 Route de Montfavet 84000 Avignon. Tel: +33 4 90 82 40 27.*

Arles

The city in which Van Gogh was at his most productive is steeped in Provençal culture. Roman ruins abound, including an amazingly preserved amphitheatre.

Getting there
Car- Paris (6 hrs 45), Marseille (1 hr), Lyon (2 hrs 45), Nimes (35 mins).
Train- Paris- the best way to get to Arles from Paris is using train and bus via Avignon. The journey takes around 4 hrs (from €53). Marseille- 45 mins (from €10), Nimes 30 mins (from €7.10), Lyon- 2 hrs (from €28).

See & Do
Roman ruins such as the amphitheatre (**les Arènes d'Arles**) and the **Classical theatre** are well worth visiting, even if only from the outside. Cultural events are held at both venues, with events at the theatre viewable from outside the gates.
If the **winding streets** feel strangely familiar, it's not déjà vu; **Van Gough** painted the town frequently during his time here. The yellow house that he lived in was unfortunately destroyed in the Second World War, but there is a **trail marked by plaques** that can be followed if you want to follow in Vincent's footsteps. A brochure can be picked up at the tourist office.

Sleep

Logis Hotel de la Muette, *15 rue des Suisses, 13200 Arles-* A cosy boutique hotel with central spiral staircase and open stone walls. Centrally located on a small square in the old town, 15 minutes walk from the train station. Wine stores, laundry, cafes and restaurants are all close by. Rooms are large and comfortable and the breakfast is fantastic (from €89).

Best Western Atrium Arles, *1 Rue Emile Fassin, Les Lices, 13200 Arles-* Superb location, 10 minutes walk from the main attractions. There is a small swimming pool up on the roof with excellent views of the city. Car parking with plenty of space and easy to get in and out by road (from €65).

Vets

Clinical Veterinary Remparts, *26 Boulevard Emile Combes, 13200 Arles. Tel: +33 4 90 96 64 06.*

Clinical Veterinary Alyscamps, *Arches Avenue, Zone Fourchon, 13200 Arles. Tel: +33 4 90 96 02 00.*

Worth a visit

Mont Ventoux is legendary as the scene of one of the most gruelling climbs in the Tour de France. The 1910-m high conical peak can be ascended in a car and lies 60km north-west of Avignon. With its altitude and the cooling Mistral wind, it's often snow-capped in April, while the cherry orchards below are in blossom and the fields are turning green.

Verdon Gorge- If you are travelling in a car you could take a drive along the D952 on the north rim of the Verdon Gorge, Europe's "Grand Canyon". The gorge is around 2 hrs 30 from Marseille, 1 hr 45 from St Tropez and 2 hrs from Nice. From the north rim you can check out the numerous vantage points along the way. Hiking is possible but dogs must be kept on a leash. Some of the trails forbid dogs for safety reasons, as they have ladders to climb along the route.

Monastery Saint-Paul-de-Mausole near Saint-Rémy-de-Provence is the psychiatric hospital where Vincent Van Gogh incarcerated himself for a year just before his death. The part of the hospital where Van Gogh stayed is open to the public. Van Gogh painted some of his most famous paintings during his time here and it makes a fascinating and poignant day trip. They even allowed our dog in when we visited.

Côte D'Azure

Marseille

With around one million inhabitants, Marseille is the second largest city in France. The city used to have a terrible reputation but has worked hard to reinvent itself and has now shaken off the sleaziness and danger to attract a wide range of visitors. It is also something of a cultural melting pot, which can feel more like Africa than Europe in parts.

Getting there
Car- Paris-7 hrs, Lyon- 3 hrs, Nice- 2 hrs, Nimes- 1 hr 30, Avignon- 1 hr 10.
Train- Paris- 3 hrs (€25), Marne la Vallee- 3 hrs (from €20), Lille- 4 hrs 30- (from €59), Lyon- 1 hr 45 (from €10).
Note:
Getting around Marseille can be problematic with a dog as the metropolitan transport system only allows service dogs and small dogs in carriers. It's also a nightmare to drive in the narrow, winding streets of the city centre, not to mention expensive parking. It is possible to get around the city on foot but if you're arriving by train it's probably best to stay near the station and if arriving by car to park and stay as close to the Vieux port as you can. One other option would be to stay out of the city and use the TER rail system to visit on a day trip. Good options include Aix-en Provence, Arles and Cassis.

See & Do

Vieux Port (old harbour)- With two fortresses guarding the entrance this is a picturesque spot to sit with a coffee and watch the city's street life. A free ferry shuttles passengers from one side of the port to the other.

Notre Dame de la Garde- The domed basilica overlooks the city from a hilltop south of the Vieux Port. Fishermen used to have their boats blessed here and you can still see many boat models hanging around in the church. Walk to the church from the Vieux Port (30 minutes) and enjoy spectacular views of the city. There is also a tourist train from the Vieux Port to reach the church.

Le Panier- The oldest area of the town with narrow winding streets and colourful old houses. In the middle of this area there is the Vielle Charité, a wonderful old monument, now hosting museums and exhibitions.

Beaches in Marseille are not always great. However the small beaches south of the city centre between La Pointe Rouge harbour and La Madrague harbour are cleaner, nicer and usually slightly less crowded.

Noailles- The area around the Noailles subway station is lined with Arabic and Indo-Chinese shops. Some of the streets could be part of a bazaar in North Africa.

La Corniche- A walkway and a road by the sea that provides lovely views of the coast, the **Château** d'If to the south, and les Calanques to the east.

The Calanques- A series of miniature fjords to the south of Marseille where the limestone cliffs plunge into the azure sea. The easiest Calanques to access without a private vehicle are the ones near Cassis. Take a local TER train to Cassis, then follow the path along the seafront to Port Miou.

Château d'If- Built on a small island near the city, initially as a fort and later a prison. It is best known as the prison in the novel *The Count of Monte Cristo* Tourist boats leave from the Vieux Port.

Sleep
New Hotel St Charles, *4 Allees Leon Gambetta, 13001 Marseille*- Close to Gare St Charles and two more metro and tram stations - Noailles and Réformés-Canebière. It's one of the better hotels in the vicinity of Gare St Charles with large and comfortable rooms, but the area isn't the best in Marseille. A decent option if you're travelling by rail and want a convenient hotel. Rates are cheaper on weekends and there are regular promotions (from €60).

Adagio Marseille Vieux Port, *30 rue Jean Trinquet, 13002 Marseille-* Not exactly central but only 15 minutes walk from the Vieux Port and with a car park (paid) this is a decent option for people arriving by car. The rooms are spacious and with a kitchenette. Rooms from €90.

Radisson Blu Hotel, Marseille Vieux Port, *38-40 Quai de Rive Neuve, 13007 Marseille-* Right on the Vieux Port so great for walking to all the nearby attractions. Rooms are spacious and comfortable with fantastic views of the port (ask for a view when booking) but the pool and gym aren't great. The parking situation (like most of Marseille) is dire. The hotel is next to a 24 hour car park but it'll cost you €22 for 24 hours. Rooms from €120.

Vets

Rapoport Frederic, *22 Rue de la Loge, 13002 Marseille.* Tel: +33 4 91 90 99 96.

Clinical Veterinary Sainte - Dr De Michiel, *83 Rue Sainte, 13007 Marseille.* Tel: +33 4 91 54 33 80.

Sci Jules Verne, *22 Rue de la Loge, 13002 Marseille.* Tel: +33 4 91 90 99 96.

Nice

Capital of the Riviera **Nice** is more than just a beach resort. It is also a major city with fantastic shopping, restaurants and bars. There is a picturesque old town and you'll see designer dogs everywhere you go, but there is also the crime and traffic that come with any other metropolis.

Getting there
Car- Paris-8 hrs, Lyon- 4 hrs 30, Marseille- 2 hrs.
Train- Paris- 6 hrs (from €41), Lyon- 4 hrs 30 (from €40), Marseille- 2 hrs 30 (from €22).
The **Lunea** night train runs from Paris to Nice. Dogs are permitted onboard as long as they are muzzled and on a leash. However private compartments are available for one two or three people and if you have a **private compartment** there is **no need to muzzle or leash** your dog.

See & Do
The **Colline du Château** overlooking the Baie des Anges and harbour has spectacular views over the city. Not much is left of its ruined **castle** besides crumbling walls. Still, climbing up the stairs to reach the platforms 90 metres above Nice is well worth the view.
The **old town (Vieux Nice)** is a maze of streets and alleys, with many picturesque houses, boutiques, restaurants and galleries.
Cliff Walk- Past the old port toward Monaco there is a beautiful walk along a pathway around the Cap de Nice. The path leads from **Coco Beach** halfway to

Villefranche. Be prepared for a lot of steps.

Promenade des Anglais- Created in the nineteenth-century by the English residents for afternoon strolls along the seafront. Nowadays cyclists, skateboarders, in-line-skaters, baby strollers and whole families can be seen out for a stroll along the Promenade. The Promenade has numerous blue chairs (*chaises bleues*) and cabanas along it, which are perfect for a rest and watching the azure waters of the **Bay of Angels (*la Baie des Anges*)**.

Nice has a designated area of **beach** for dogs at the far end of the **Baie des Anges**. The beach is at **Carras**, near the airport which is a long but pleasant stroll along the Promenade des Anglais. There are plenty of hotel rooms located in this area.

Sleep

Radisson Blu Nice, *223 Promenade des Anglais, 06200 Nice-* Beautiful rooms with large spacious bathrooms. Ideally located at the beginning of the Promenade des Anglais, many rooms have sea views (rooms from €95).

Mercure Nice Promenade des Anglais, *2 rue Halevy, 06000 Nice-* Excellent location across the road from the Promenade des Anglais. Vieux Nice is less than a ten minute walk and there are many restaurants close to the hotel. The train station is a 10-12 minute walk. Clean and functional Mercure style rooms, some of which have a sea view (from €120).

ibis Style Nice Aeroport, *127 boulevard Rene Cassin, 06200 Nice-* Clean and functional hotel rooms, close to the airport and Saint Augustin train station, so handy for trains to Monaco and Cannes. The Promenade des

Anglais stretches as far as the hotel and the city centre is a pleasant 20 minute walk along the seafront. There is a dog friendly beach nearby (rooms from €65).

Vets

Clinical veterinary castle-Boube Olivier, *2 Place Guynemer, 06300 Nice. Tel: +33 4 93 26 10 00. Near the port.*

SCP Fabienne Guillemin, *85 Boulevard Gambetta, 06000 Nice. Tel: +33 4 97 14 80 13. Near the train station.*

Clinical Veterinary Cap Sud, *173 Bis Avenue Sainte-Marguerite, 06000 Nice. Tel: +33 4 93 71 02 79. Near the airport.*

Cannes

Until recently Cannes was a small fishing village, however it's now one of the most glamorous coastal towns in Europe. Famous as the venue for the Cannes Film Festival, in May, during which time you can see actors, celebrities, and directors up close and in person on the famous steps of the **Palais des Festivals** at the end of La Croisette.

Getting there
Car- As with St Tropez, Monaco and other towns on the French Riviera, access by road at popular times can be slow and frustrating. The coast roads are generally packed, and there are few ways to descend from inland. Parking at Nice, Mougins or Mouans Sartoux and using the train is the best idea.

Trains - SNCF trains run between Nice's St. Augustine station and Cannes every 30 minutes. The journey takes 30 minutes and costs €11-15 (round-trip). The views are amazing as the train runs adjacent the beach.

See & Do
Old town- Narrow winding streets filled with restaurants and souvenir shops. The view from the castle ruins at the top is excellent.

Covered Market (Marché Forville)- From roughly 8:00 am until 12:30pm, Tues-Sunday, you can wonder the aisles of this amazing market to purchase hand crafted cheeses, fresh fish, local olives and olive oils, herbs, eggs, meats, glorious produce, fresh flowers, honey, pates and more. Surrounding the market there are also terrific shops specialising in numerous food items. You'll see many a dog taking its master for a stroll here.

Palais des Festivals- Where stars of the screen gather and watch films every May during the festival. Europe's equivalent of the Oscars. You won't be able to resist posing for a photograph on the 22 steps leading up to the entrance.

Port- Admire the yachts of the rich and famous.

La Croisette- the centre of the city's tourist activity, a promenade along the seafront, where many a designer dog can be spotted with its owner in tow.

Îles de Lérins- Two islands in the bay that are definitely worth visiting. St Honorat is the smaller of the two and has a monastery and ruined castle. Ste Marguerite also has a castle, shops, bars, and restaurants. Both are a haven from the hustle and bustle of Cannes. Dogs are allowed on the ferry and on the island. Find a quiet cove, some shade from palm trees, and swim with your dog around the rocky coves. A return ticket costs €11-13 with ferries departing every hour roughly from 7am until 5:30pm.

Festival de Cannes- The famous film festival takes place in mid-May every year and the world's biggest celebrities descend on Cannes to walk the red carpet. So too, however, do thousands of tourists, hoping to catch a glimpse of their idols.

Sleep
Good quality hotels in Cannes are very expensive. Even basic hotels such as Etap and Kyriad cost €75 and €150

respectively (in late October). Unless you absolutely have to stay in Cannes it is better to stay in Nice and use the train to visit.

Vets
There are vets in Cannes, but as everything is so expensive it's probably best to use one in Nice.

Worth a visit

St Tropez- Undeniably glamorous but vastly over-hyped (and a nightmare to drive to in summer) St-Tropez was, until relatively recently accessible only by boat. This had all changed by the end of the First World War and St-Tropez was an establishing itself as a **destination for artists and writers.** It was then cata-pulted to world renown when Brigitte Bardot starred here in *And God Created Woman* **and** has been filled to the rafters with tourists ever since. The beaches, though lovely are officially out of bounds for dogs in the summer months. Out of high season it's okay to take your dog on the beach and you'll more than likely see the odd dog on the beach in season. If you really want to let your dog on the beach though it's better to go to **Sainte-Maxime** across the water, where dogs have ac-cess to a dedicated stretch of the sand.

At peak periods in summer expect world-class traffic jams on the main road. Even in April, it can take a cou-ple of hours to do the final two miles. An alternative op-tion is to drive to **St Raphaël** or **Ste Maxime**, leave your car there and take the ferry across the bay. The train also stops at **Fréjus, close to St Raphaël** from where you can catch the boat.

Fréjus and **St-Raphaël-** Dating back to Roman times, with a scattering of **remains still evident**, these neigh-bouring towns boast a medieval cathedral complex, a lovely beach with a dog friendly section and a vast mari-na, **Port-Fréjus.** 1 hr 30 mins from Marseille by car or train, and around an hour from Nice by car or train.

Antibes hasn't escaped overdevelopment altogether but it has at least avoided the scale seen elsewhere on the Côte. The old town is attractive with a great **market** and seafront castle (Marseille 2 hrs, Nice 30 mins).

Menton- Between Monaco and the Italian Riviera Menton is in many ways more Italian than French. It also boasts a microclimate with 331 sunny days per year. In winter it's possible to ski in Alpes Maritime in the mornings and swim in the Mediterranean in the afternoon. Your dog might have trouble skiing, but there are at least two sections of beach where they will be welcome all year round. Menton is around 40 minutes drive from Nice but has a curious one way system, it's best to park near the port and walk, or use one of the regular trains from Nice (30 mins).

Monaco

The principality of Monaco is a tiny state close to the Italian Riviera. Monaco is the second smallest independent state in the world (around the size of London's Hyde Park) and is almost entirely urban. It has been ruled since the 13th Century by the Grimaldi family and is best known for the Formula One Grand Prix and as a tax haven for the rich and famous.

Getting there
Car- Besides the A8, which runs from Monaco to Nice and Marseille (30 mins and 2 hrs 30 respectively), there also three more scenic roads: the Basse Corniche (Low Coast-Road - Highway 98), along the sea, the Moyenne Corniche (Middle Coast Road - Highway 7) and the Grande Corniche (Great Coast Road). All are spectacular drives offering views over the coast line.
Rail- The Monaco-Monte Carlo station has 2-4 services per hour to Nice (15 mins, €4), Cannes and beyond.

See & Do
Monaco-Ville is still an old perched village at heart and an astonishingly picturesque site. It is made up almost entirely of old pedestrian streets and passages.
Palais Princier (Prince's Palace) offers a panoramic view overlooking the Port and Monte-Carlo. Every day just before noon visitors gather to watch the changing of the guard at the front of the palace.

Monaco Cathedral a Romanesque-Byzantine church dedicated to Saint Nicolas and where the remains of former Princes of Monaco and Princess Grace (Kelly) are buried.

La Condamine- Marvel at the luxurious yachts and cruise ships in the marina.

Dogs are banned from green spaces in Monaco, except for designated canine zones (*espaces canins*) below:

Monaco City: the area of St. Martin's Gardens near the Oceaongraphic museum

Monte Carlo: the area of Avenue de Grande Bretagne opposite the Trocadéro

Fontvieille: behind the ticket office in the Chapiteau of Monaco

Fontvieille: in front of the Zone A housing area

Fontvieille: the gardens next to Fontvieille school

Moneghetti: Lamarck Square

Parcours Vita: Park on Hector Otto Avenue

Avenue Pasteur, behind the Villa Pasteur, in the area opposite the entrance to the cemetery

Dogs are permitted to relieve themselves in these areas, but any droppings must be disposed of in litter bins. For this purpose, the Department of Urban Management (*Direction de l'Aménagement Urbain*) has placed waste disposal bag dispensers around the eight parks.

Sleep

If you're on a budget, Monaco is not the best place to be. It's better to stay in Nice or one of the other along the Côte. You could even stay across the border on the Italian Riviera.

If you must stay in Monaco and want a decent quality hotel:

Port Palace, *7 Avenue JF Kennedy, Monte-Carlo 98000-* A 4-star boutique hotel in Monaco overlooking Port Hercule. It offers a spa with a hot tub and hammam, just 1 km from the train station. Each room has a private dressing room and en suite bathroom complete with a whirlpool bath, bathrobe and slippers. The famous Monte-Carlo casino is just a 6-minute walk away or the hilltop palace can be found in 2 km. Private parking is possible on site and Wi-Fi is available throughout the hotel (rooms from €200 in October).

Vets

Robotti Cristina, *7 Avenue du Général de Gaulle, 06240 Beausoleil. Tel: +33 4 93 41 86 87.*

Paolo Conti, *7 Avenue du Général de Gaulle, 06240 Beausoleil. Tel: +33 4 93 41 86 87.*

Useful Phrases and websites

Vets

Can you read my pet's microchip? Do you have a microchip reader? The microchip is located here (point where the microchip is).

Pouvez-vous lire la micropuce de mon animal? Avez-vous un lecteur de micropuce? La puce est ici (montrez du doigt l'endroit où se trouve la puce).

My pet has to be treated against tapeworms (Echinococcus multilocularis). Can you do this?

Mon animal doit être traité contre les ténias (Echinococcus multilocularis). Pouvez-vous le faire?

You will need to complete section VII of my pet's passport/give me an official certificate to show that you have treated my pet. You must record the day and time that you did the treatment.

Je dois vous demander de remplir les section VII du passeport de mon animal/de me remettre un certificat officiel prouvant que vous avez traité mon animal. Vous devez indiquer le jour et l'heure du traitement.

My dog has been vaccinated against rabies.

Mon chien a été vacciné contre la rage.

My pet is not resident in France. Therefore it does not have to be tattooed.

Mon animal ne réside pas en France. Il n'a donc pas besoin d'être tatoué.

Shops, Bars and restaurants

Is my dog allowed in here?

Est-ce que les chiens sont autorisés ici?

May I have some water for my dog?

Puis-je avoir un peu d'eau pour mon chien?

Websites

Pet passport advice
https://www.gov.uk/pet-travel-information-for-pet-owners

Train tickets in France
http://www.ouigo.com/fr
http://www.idtgv.com
http://www.voyages-sncf.com

Dogs allowed beaches
http://www.tele-animaux.com/pratique,plages-autorisees-aux-animaux.html

Ferry companies and Eurotunnel
http://www.myferrylink.com
http://ldlines.co.uk
http://www.brittany-ferries.co.uk
http://www.poferries.com
http://www.condorferries.co.uk
http://www.dfdsseaways.co.uk
http://www.eurotunnel.com

Hotels
http://www.kayak.co.uk

15683527R00081

Printed in Great Britain
by Amazon